Studies in applied regional science

This series in applied regional, urban and environmental analysis aims to provide regional scientists with a set of adequate tools for empirical regional analysis and for practical regional planning problems. The major emphasis in this series will be upon the applicability of theories and methods in the field of regional science; these will be presented in a form which can be readily used by practitioners. Both new applications of existing knowledge and newly developed ideas will be published in the series.

Studies in applied regional science
Vol. 12

Editor-in-Chief

P. Nijkamp
Free University, Amsterdam

Editorial Board

Å.E Andersson
University of Gothenburg, Gothenburg
W. Isard
Regional Science Institute, Philadelphia
L.H. Klaassen
Netherlands Economic Institute, Rotterdam
I. Masser
State University, Utrecht
N. Sakashita
Osaka University, Osaka

Economies of scale in manufacturing location

Theory and measure

Gerald A. Carlino

Assistant Professor of Economics,
University of Missouri at Kansas City

Martinus Nijhoff Social Sciences Division
Leiden/Boston 1978

ISBN 90 207 0721.3

Distributors for North America
Kluwer Boston Inc.
160 Old Derby Street
Hingham, MA 02043 USA

Copyright © 1978 by H.E. Stenfert Kroese B.V., Leiden
No part of this book may be reproduced in any form by print,
photoprint, microfilm or any other means, without written
permission from the publisher

Photoset in Malta by Interprint (Malta) Ltd.

Printed in the Netherlands by Intercontinental Graphics.

For Jan

Preface

The research reported in this book began as part of a Ph.D. dissertation submitted to the University of Pittsburgh in 1976. Revisions were accomplished at Florida International University in Miami.

There have been many people who were instrumental in the formation and completion of this research. The contributions made by Jack Ochs are far too numerous to mention. Jack's insights and suggestions will always be appreciated. I am also grateful to Melvin Greenhut, David Houston, Tatsuhiko Kawashima, Asatoshi Maeshiro, William Miernyk, Josephine Olson, Peter Nijkamp and Harry Richardson who read and critically reviewed earlier manuscripts. I am doubly indebted to Harry Richardson who initially suggested this investigation. Special thanks are in order for Gene Gruver, Peter Montiel, Randy Miller and James Wheller for always finding the time to hear out many of my arguments. In addition, I appreciate the valuable suggestions they made as well.

I am grateful, moreover, to Janice Carlino who most generously gave of herself to assist in this in any way she could. Janice not only helped with data preparation and with typing entire drafts of earlier manuscripts, but, more importantly, showed an unusual degree of tolerance toward one for whom the research effort is not the most tranquil of experiences.

Finally, I would like to acknowledge Nancy Schell for her conscientious efforts in typing and editing the finalized draft.

Contents

Preface vii

1. **Introduction** 1

2. **Agglomeration economies: a survey of the literature** 6
2.1. Introduction 6
2.2. Agglomeration economies: a theoretical approach 6
2.3. Agglomeration economies: an empirical approach 14
2.4. Conclusion 28

3.1. **Agglomeration and location of manufacturing activity: the theoretical framework** 30
3.1. Introduction 30
3.2. Central place theory and agglomeration 30
3.3. The theoretical framework 38
3.3.1. Internal scale economies 41
3.3.2. Localization economies 42
3.3.3. Urbanization economies 43
3.4. The technique of measuring agglomeration forces: the model 44
3.4.1. Technical change 46
3.4.2. Returns to scale 48
3.4.3. Specifying the functional form 49
3.4.4. The empirical model 54
3.5. Conclusion 59

4. **The empirical investigation** 60
4.1. Introduction 60
4.2. Estimating scale economies: the time-series model 60
4.3. Decomposition: the cross-sectional model 75
4.3.1. SIC 20 food and kindred products 82
4.3.2. SIC 22 textile mill products 83
4.3.3. SIC 23 apparel and related products 83
4.3.4. SIC 24 lumber and wood products 85
4.3.5. SIC 25 furniture and fixtures 85

4.3.6.	SIC 26 paper and allied products	86
4.3.7.	SIC 27 printing and publishing	87
4.3.8.	SIC 28 chemicals and allied products	88
4.3.9.	SIC 29 petroleum and coal products	89
4.3.10.	SIC 30 rubber and plastic products (N.E.C.)	90
4.3.11.	SIC 31 leather and leather products	91
4.3.12.	SIC 32 stone, clay and glass products	91
4.3.13.	SIC 33 primary metal industries	92
4.3.14.	SIC 34 fabricated metal products	93
4.3.15.	SIC 35 machinery, except electrical	93
4.3.16.	SIC 36 electrical machinery	94
4.3.17.	SIC 37 transportation equipment	94
4.3.18.	SIC 38 instruments and related products	95
4.3.19.	SIC 39 miscellaneous manufacturing	96
4.4.	Generalization of the empirical results	96

5. Conclusion 98

Appendix A 103

Appendix B 107

References 108

1. Introduction

The objective of this research is the extension of empirically validated knowledge of the forces of agglomeration on manufacturing activity.

The analytical aspect of this problem can be described as follows: manufacturing activity is neither spread evenly nor in a continuous fashion over the national economy. Generally, economic activity tends to be concentrated in comparatively few urbanized places. Locational theorists, beginning with Weber (1929) and continuing with Hoover (1937) and Isard (1956) have emphasized the relative importance of agglomeration economies in explaining the concentration of economic activity, especially industry activity, in metropolitan areas. To be sure, the concentration of manufacturing activity is in part accounted for by gravitation towards either localized raw materials (material orientation) or larger concentrations of population (market orientation). The point is, however, that the observed concentration of industry suggests the influence of systematic forces other than material and/or market orientation.

In particular, for any theory which attempts to explain the spatial concentration of production, the introduction of agglomeration economies, which are based upon indivisible factors of production or production processes, is essential. These indivisibilities (the advantages associated with large-scale activities) do not permit proportionality to be maintained at all levels of production between all inputs in the production process, and lead to increasing returns to scale.

Since our view has it that agglomeration economies are technical in nature (founded upon indivisibilities), production function techniques are a useful tool for econometric analysis. Economists, when estimating production functions, usually assume that most scale economies are realized within a particular plant.[1] The purpose of this work, however, is to consider the advantages of scale economies writ large, i.e., internal as well as external economies.

The effects which are included under the heading external economies arise both from *intra*industry clustering on the one hand, and the more general case of *inter*industry concentration on the other. The former have been christened localization economies, while the latter are known as urbanization economies.

To sum, agglomeration economies are seen as being composed of internal and external economies of scale, both of which are consequent upon indivisibilities. Given this orientation, we will employ such terms as agglomeration economies, total scale economies, the total scale parameter, the scale coefficient and the scale parameter interchangeably. Likewise, when we speak more narrowly of external economies, this refers to either localization economies, urbanization economies, or some combination of the two.

The industrial classification chosen is the Standard Industrial Classification (SIC) system. The SIC system was developed for use in the classification of establishments by type of activity engaged in; for purposes of facilitating the collection, tabulation, presentation, and analysis of data relating to establishments; and for promoting uniformity and comparability in the presentation of statistical data collected by various agencies of the United States Government, state agencies, trade associations, and private research organizations. The SIC system breaks all industries down into major industrial groups having a two-digit designation and subdivides each group into component major industries (three-digit designation) which are further subdivided into specific industries (four-digit designation). The system extends to the seven-digit level for some industries.

Much of the available U.S. data on manufacturing activity and most of that which are comparable among urban areas on a nationwide basis, come from the U.S. Census of Manufactures. One of the geographical concepts used to collect and report the data is the standard metropolitan statistical area, or SMSA. An SMSA includes one central city (or possibly twin cities) of at least 50,000 residents, and one or more contiguous counties which are metropolitan in character, as determined by the percentage of the labor force which is nonagricultural and by the amount of commuting between the county and the city. There existed 233 SMSA's as of July 1, 1970, however, our study could only include industries located in 68 of these due to data availability. The 68 SMSA's comprising this study are given in Appendix B.

In order to estimate the scale parameters, time-series data were fitted to a production function relationship. Specifically, the scale coefficients were estimated for the various two-digit manufacturing industries in each of our 68 SMSA's, where data were available. This provides us with a series of estimated scale coefficients for a given industry across SMSA's.

At this level of generality, however, all that we have are numerous estimates of the *total* scale parameters for the establishments in the industry under consideration. To be sure, the components contributing to total scale differ by industry. The total scale coefficients for establishments in some industries could best be explained, for example, by localization economies, while in others urbanization economies could be important, still in others some combination of urbanization and localization could be at work. This suggests that these total scale measures would be more meaningful if we could disaggregate them by industry, into the relevant contribution contributed by: (1) large scale economies; (2) localization economies; (3) urbanization economies; and (4) urbanization diseconomies. For this purpose cross-sectional analysis is employed. That is, the total scale coefficients estimated in the time-series study are employed as dependent variables in an industry-by-industry cross sectional model. The various cross-sectional models will then decompose the total scale measure into the various agglomeration forces.

There are a number of reasons why a study of this sort contributes to both the discipline, as well as to various groups in society. It is widely believed by regional scientists that agglomeration forces are of paramount importance in an explanation of the location of manufacturing industry. While these agglomeration tendencies are well defined in the existing urban/regional literature, they have not been adequately measured. As the survey chapter (Chapter 2) of this work illustrates, most of the empirical attempts have been indirect rather than direct (i.e., developing proxies designed to capture the agglomeration effect). Not only have the existing measurement techniques been indirect, but they have also isolated on a partial measure of scale (e.g., measuring the localization component only), or they have been highly aggregated (i.e., lumping all the various forces together in a single number).

This research has a contribution to make to the existing literature on optimal city size with respect to agglomeration of manufacturing activity. The optimal city size studies to date operate under the hypothesis that larger concentrations of economic activity offer external economies, which are offset somewhat by diseconomies of scale, to many firms. The question which naturally arises then is whether or not an optimal size exists? Optimal in the sense that the net urbanization economies (urbanization economies less urbanization diseconomies) are at a maximum. To do this, however, a measure of both urbanization economies as well as diseconomies is required. Many of the optimal city size studies employ population scale of cities of different sizes as proxy for these measures. The justification for employing population scale as a proxy for urbanization economies and diseconomies is based on theoretical grounds only. In a later chapter of this work we will demonstrate the weakness of this theoretical proposition.

Not only is population scale a poor proxy to use to capture the effects of business agglomeration economies, but the optimal city size must vary for different industry clusters. It is this point which is glossed over in many of the optimal city size studies undertaken thus far. Typically, one and only one optimal population size is estimated. Even if we overlooked the fact that population scale is a poor proxy for urbanization economies, surely the optimal population size must be different for establishments in food and kindred products than for establishments in textile mill products, for example. More will be said on the optimal city size question in ensuing chapters.

Given this background it is easy to see the major contribution of this work. Our measurement technique is, first of all, a more direct measure of the agglomeration or total scale parameter. In addition, an effort will be made to disaggregate these estimated total scale parameters into the various agglomeration forces, by industry.

Furthermore, quantitative estimates of scale economies are required for several other purposes. The agglomeration forces are one stimuli contributing to the growth of the economy, and estimates of these forces are required to find out more about the sources of growth. Entrepreneurs require a knowledge of scale economies as this is one of the factors which determines the optimum method of organizing production. Research to determine scale economies is required to provide information which will shed some light on the results of government economic policies, e.g., regulations governing monopolies, tax concessions to small firms, and incentives to firms to establish new plants in developing regions.

INTRODUCTION 5

In closing this introductory chapter, we would like to sketch an overview of the following chapters. The next chapter provides a survey, both theoretical and empirical, with respect to the existing agglomeration literature. This chapter serves also as a basis upon which the theoretical chapter, Chapter 3, is built. In Chapter 4 we econometrically estimated the model developed in Chapter 3. Finally, Chapter 5 serves as a concluding chapter considering the policy implications of this volume as well as offering suggestions for further research.

NOTE

1. Strictly speaking, economies of scale and increasing returns to scale are related, but they are not one in the same. Increasing returns to scale are only the technological component of economies of scale. Another component of economies of scale may be derived from pecuniary effects. We will, however, use increasing returns to scale and economies of scale interchangeably.

2. Agglomeration economies: a survey of the literature

2.1 INTRODUCTION

Generally, agglomeration economies refer to the external economies associated with size and concentration. The benefits of size and concentration vary for different cross-sections of the urban population. Three such groupings may be identified:

1. *Consumer agglomeration economies*: larger concentrations of population can provide consumers with greater variety of goods and services than do smaller ones. For example, our largest cities can support professional sports, theater, opera and the symphony. In addition, they offer health, educational and welfare services, the availability of job opportunities, a complete range of medical and dental services, etc.
2. *Business agglomeration economies*: intra-industry concentration and/or metropolitan locations offer many advantages to business firms, some of which are greater the larger the intra-industry cluster and/or the larger the city. Examples of these are taken up in the following section and will therefore not be discussed here.
3. *Social agglomeration economies*: which affect all groups in society, although somewhat differently. Probably the most pre-eminent example under this heading is efficiency in public services.

2.2 AGGLOMERATION ECONOMIES: A THEORETICAL APPROACH

Since the objective of this work is an understanding of the forces of agglomeration on the concentration of manufacturing activity we will take up in the ensuing sections a more complete discussion of the development and measurement of business agglomeration economies.

Advantages of an urban location accruing to business firms have long been recognized by economists. In fact, Alfred Marshall (1966:365–366) argues that the advantages of urban locations frequently dwarf internal economies of scale:

... we have seen how the economies which result from a high industrial organization often depend only to a small extent on the resources of individual firms. Those internal economies which each establishment has to arrange for itself are frequently very small as compared to those external economies which result from the general progress of the industrial environment; the situation of a business nearly always plays a great part in determining the extent to which it can avail itself of external economies; and the situation value which a site derives from the growth of a rich and active population close to it, or from the opening up of railways and other good means of communication with existing markets, is the most striking of all the influences which changes in the industrial environment exert on cost of production.

The introduction of agglomeration economies into the literature of regional analysis has been credited to Alfred Weber (1929). Weber assumed: (1) given locations of raw materials; (2) fixed locations and sizes of individual places of consumption; (3) uniform transportation costs per ton mile, which he divided into assembly costs incurred in transporting raw materials to the point of production and marketing costs incurred in transporting the commodity to market; (4) that labor is immobile, that wages are fixed, and the supply of labor at that wage rate is unlimited, but wages vary from place to place; (5) an inelastic demand for products; (6) fixed technical coefficients; and (7) cost minimization. In short, Weber attempted to discover the forces which ultimately would be responsible for location of a manufacturing establishment. Therefore, he first sought a regional location on the basis of minimum transportation costs, then adjusted that location for differences in labor costs, and finally added considerations of agglomeration, i.e., that two production units in the same industry could incur economies from spatial juxtaposition.

Weber distinguished between two types of transportation costs – assembly costs and marketing costs. The former represent those costs incurred in transporting raw materials to the point of production; the latter are the costs incurred in transporting the final product to market. Raw materials can be divided into ubiquitous and localized material. Ubiquitous raw materials can by definition, be obtained anywhere. Therefore, they do not involve transportation costs to move them to the point of production. Localized raw materials will, however, involve no transfer cost only if the production point is located at their point of occurrence.

Two further terms need to be introduced. The first of these is the material index, defined as the ratio of the weight of the used localized materials to the weight of the final product. Weber also used the concept of locational weight, which may be expressed as the ratio of the weight of the product (W_p) plus the weight of the localized material per unit of product (W_L) to the weight of the product. Thus, the locational weight can be expressed as:

$$L = \frac{W_p + W_L}{W_p} = \frac{W_p}{W_p} + \frac{W_L}{W_p}$$

but W_L/W_p is just the material index (M), so $L = 1 + M$. The locational weight has a minimum value of unity when the material index is zero, i.e., when only ubiquitous raw materials are employed. If $1 \leq L < 2$, the production is said to be a weight gaining activity, since the localized materials needed to produce one unit of output weighs less than the weight of one unit of product. Weight gaining activities tend, *ceteris paribus*, to be market oriented. If, however, $L > 2$, production is characterized as weight losing and, *ceteris paribus*, weight losing activities tend to be input oriented.

Another Weberian concept which must be introduced is the notion of an isodapane. Assume a plant is located at its minimum-transport cost (MTC) location (P_1). If the plant moves away from P_1, it must necessarily incur greater transfer costs. The further it moves away, the greater the difference will be over and above the minimum. We can locate all points which exceed MTC by an equal amount and join them by a curve. This curve is called the isodapane. That is, the isodapane consists of the loci of points of equal transport costs about the MTC site. Necessarily then, we have a series of such isodapanes for all values of transport cost around the MTC point (P_1), assuming transportation is possible in all directions.

Consider the case of labor orientation. For labor to draw the plant away from the MTC site, the savings in labor cost must exceed (or at least equal) the additional costs above the MTC. As we get farther away from the minimum, there will be an isodapane beyond which the increased transport costs cannot be offset by labor economies. Weber christened this the critical isodapane. Within (that is, on) the critical isodapane, savings in labor costs offset the increased transportation costs; outside it they do not. Hence, within the critical isodapane firms will be labor-oriented; outside it they will be transport-cost-oriented.

Thus far we have followed the Weberian method of determining the MTC location of firms in isolation. Decisions regarding the location of an individual firm usually involve, however, consideration of the location of other firms. External economies of scale can be obtained as a result of spatial concentration of industrial firms at a particular point. These economies of association derive from the specialized division of labor between plants, better repair facilities, a specialized labor organization, the development of markets for the materials and products of an industry, and the lowering of social overhead cost. The only decentralizing force is rent, which is related to the size of the cluster.

Consider fig. 2.1 where we have two production units (P_1 and P_2) each of which is located at its MTC point. Suppose agglomeration economies from locating these two units together can be gained at an alternative site. Whether or not agglomeration occurs depends upon the intersection or non-intersection of the critical isodapanes. If the critical isodapane for P_1 is I_{11} and if for P_2 it is I_{22}, agglomeration is not feasible and both would remain at their minimum cost sites. This is so because the cost savings obtainable from spatial juxtaposition would be more than offset by increased transfer costs. If, however, the critical isodapanes intersect (i.e., I_{12} for P_1, and I_{21} for P_2), agglomeration could then take place at a site within the common shaded segment. To see this, let us assume that both firms could cut their production costs by $5.00 per unit if both of them operated in the same location, taking advantage of economies of agglomeration. In order to gain from this, however, a firm must not incur more than $5.00 in additional transportation costs. In fig. 2.1, I_{21} and I_{12} represent the critical isodapanes for each firm. The shaded area is the only place where plants can locate together and still each incur less than $5.00 of additional transport costs. Agglomeration is thus possible here. However, all points within the common segment are possible agglomeration sites, since production at any of these points is cheaper than at individual MTC locations. The question then becomes, which is the optimal site?

From P_1's point of view point A is the optimal site since this would minimize its deviations from its MTC site. However, location at site A maximizes firm P_2's deviation from its MTC site and hence it would opt for location at point B instead. Weber's solution to this problem was to argue that the optimal site is that site which offers the lowest transport cost for the total combined output. That is to say, the larger of the two units of production will attract the smaller unit to its optimal site, since this minimizes the total devisions from MTC points.

While Weber's work is pathbreaking, it is nonetheless subject to serious criticism. To begin with, industrial development, to some extent, is a historical process. Plants which have already been located exhibit considerable inertia, due to heavy relocation costs. Therefore, as new plants come into existence, they tend to agglomerate around these established points of production, thereby strengthening and reinforcing the gravitational pull of these points. What this suggests is that an evolutionary framework becomes quite critical as a locational factor; and substitutional models which do not account for historical regional structure are of limited significance.

Isard and Smith (1967) and Stevens (1967) have demonstrated, however, that Weber's derivation of the optimal site within the common segment is unsatisfactory, even if plants were completely mobile. The actual site of agglomeration depends upon the resolution of the conflict of interests of the location decision makers. This

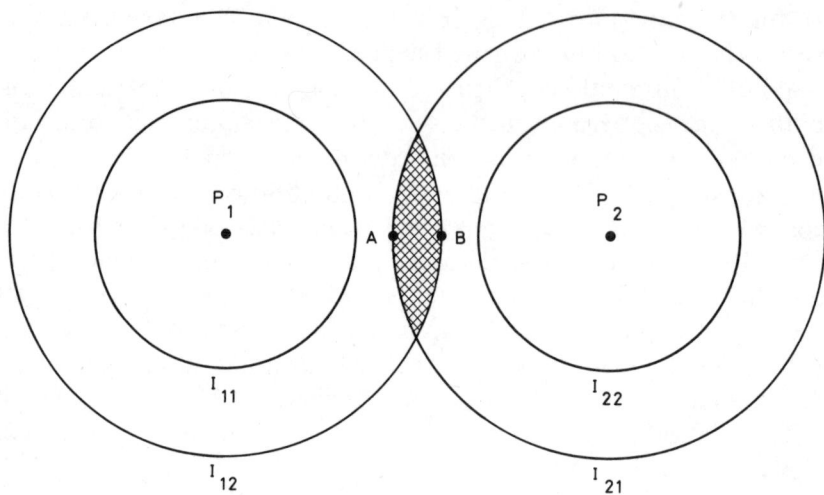

Fig. 2.1.

in turn depends upon concession on the part of each decision maker, and concession is determined by bargaining power and/or ability.

Returning to the concept of a critical isodapancy Paelinck and Nijkamp (1975:38) have pointed out just how unclear this notion is in Weber's approach. 'There is no guarantee, that there exists only one unique critical isodapane, since the spatial pattern of wage differences may possess completely arbitrary forms and is not necessarily grouped in a regular way around the minimum-cost point P.' For a more extensive criticism of these and related points, consult Paelinck and Nijkamp and/or Isard (1956).

A more relevant criticism for our purposes is that the location of a firm results not only from evaluating the benefits and costs of locating near other plants in its industry but also by evaluating the benefits and cost associated with locating near other types of economic activity as well. Indeed, Hoover criticizes Weber's notion of agglomeration since it inextricably mingled three quite distinct forces upon local production costs:[1]

1. *Large-scale economies* within a firm consequent upon the enlargement of the firms's scale of production at one point.
2. *Localization economies* for all the firms in a single industry at a single location, consequent upon the enlargement of the total output of that industry at that location.
3. *Urbanization economies* for all firms in all industries at a single location, consequent upon the enlargement of the total economic size (population, income, output, or wealth) of that location, for all industries taken together.

The forces of agglomeration have been widely acknowledged to be of paramount importance in the development and growth of metropolitan regions. Therefore, we will now attempt a further articulation of how these forces influence production cost of the firm.

Large-scale economies are economies of scale which are *internal* to a particular firm. Generally, economists agree that in each industry with given technology and factor costs there is an optimum size of plant. It is the plant which, if operated at full capacity, would give the lowest average total cost of production. Likewise, economies of scale can be considered from the production function point of view. The production function describe the technically maximum output obtainable, with a given technology, from given quantities of inputs. Thus, whenever inputs are increased, say 5 percent, and the resulting output increases by more than 5 percent, we may conclude that economies of scale exist. The possibility for fully exploiting internal scale economies is enhanced in metropolitan places due to their relatively larger product demand.

Localization economies characterize economies *external* to the firm but *internal* to the industry. These agglomeration advantages for firms in the same industry are also important to industrial location and regional development. Indeed, numerous agglomeration advantages for firms in the same industry have been cited. Some of the more obvious include gravitation to raw material sources or to non-transportable inputs; the ability to support and have access to research and development facilities or to specialized brokers which develop to serve the needs of the industry; the development of a skilled labor pool; the development of and access to organized exchanges and specialized storage facilities which permit firms to buy on short notice thereby reducing inventory costs. More favorable freight rates are likely to be established at concentrated places of production. Intraindustry concentration could result in localization diseconomies as well. Spatial juxtaposition of plants in the same industry could result in higher wages and/or increased rents.

Since localization economies are related to scale they are more likely to influence the locational decision of small firms because large firms can create their own scale economies internally.[2] This suggests that the boundary between internal economies of large-scale production and localization economies may be quite blurred.

Urbanization economies are economies both to the firm and the industry, i.e., advantages to firms in all industries as a result of increases in total economic size at a given location. Urbanization economies include the development of large and varied labor pools; access to a larger market; the existence of entrepreneurial talent; the presence of wholesaling facilities in urban areas which reduces the level of inventories firms need on hand; the existence of commercial, financial, and banking facilities; the opportunities for face-to-face contact with specialized business services such as accountants, advertising firms and business consultants; the existence of social, cultural and leisure facilities which influence location decisions (e.g., varied restaurant cuisines, spectator sports and the Arts); and efficiency in public services (both with regard to the level of property taxes and charges for public utilities such as water).

For reasons of this kind, the advantages of urban locations are overwhelming for many firms and large centers offer external economies not found in small ones. Large concentrations, however, incur pecuniary diseconomies such as a higher wage bill, rising land values, and traffic congestion costs. For example, increased congestion tends to increase transport costs of material to and output from the plant. As a result, there has been a tendency for decentralization of industrial activity from the metropolitan central business district to the fringe of the metropolitan area. Likewise, density has a similar impact as congestion on the decentralization of economic activity because of the high rents on more centralized land.

It has also been pointed out by Greenhut (1956) and Weber (1972) that agglomeration forces tend to be reinforced in conditions of uncertainty. Since events are uncertain and new firms are typically small, they must rely upon the external economies large metropolitan areas offer. In addition, large metropolitan areas offer advantages over smaller ones because of their favourable position with respect to the production and diffusion of innovations. Evidence has been presented which indicates that the spatial diffusion of innovations begins in the largest urban areas and then tends to be transmitted down along the urban hierarchy.[3] Furthermore, location decision-makers are uncertain about the structure of future spatial costs and prices. In an uncertain world, the attractiveness of large urban centers as sites for new firms is greater than in a certain world. Risk aversion will reinforce the advantages of already established locations rather than new, untried, ones. The uncertainty and incomplete information which characterize location decisions serve to reinforce the attractiveness of centers of agglomeration of economic activity.

Chinitz argues that external economies are greater in areas where industrial structures are competitive (1961). Essentially, he reacts against the influence of scale by attempting to relate economies to market organization and industry structure. He sets forth the following tentative hypothesis: there are more entrepreneurs per dollar of output in competitive as opposed to oligopolistic industries; small firms stand a better chance of securing loans in their home locality due to less uncertainty on the part of lending institutions there than elsewhere. Furthermore, if the industrial organization in a small firm's area is competitive rather than oligopolistic, its ability to borrow is enhanced; if there is a dominant industry in an area, its wage levels influence other industries; and since large firms create so many of their auxiliary services internally, these auxiliary services may not be available externally in oligopolistic environments with the consequence that new firms must start big.

2.3. AGGLOMERATION ECONOMIES: AN EMPIRICAL APPROACH

The preceding section attempted to define agglomeration economies in terms of internal and external economies of scale. The main problems arise when we attempt to measure these forces precisely enough for use in an operational model. Most technique developed to measure the agglomeration force have been indirect (i.e., developing proxies for agglomeration) rather than direct.

An early, though unsatisfactory, technique suggested by Marcus (1965) attempted to measure agglomeration economies by industry. The underlying hypothesis of his paper is that industries sensitive to agglomeration forces will tend to develop most rapidly near areas of strong net economies. To test his hypothesis Marcus argues that growth of industry in the state of New Jersey will be influenced by the agglomerative pull of nearby New York City. His technique assumes that the expected rate of growth of the j-th industry in New Jersey ($G_{j,NJ}$) relative to the growth rate of population in New Jersey ($G_{P,NJ}$) will be equal to the ratio of these respective growth rates in the nation, i.e.,

$$\frac{G_{j,NJ}}{G_{P,NJ}} = \frac{G_{j,N}}{G_{P,N}}$$

where the subscript N = nation. If industry j in New Jersey grew at the expected rate then

$$G_{j,NJ} - G_{P,NJ}(G_{j,N}/G_{P,N}) = 0$$

If the rate of growth of industry j is, however, greater than the expected rate, Marcus suggests that this "extra" growth could be due to agglomeration economies, i.e.,

$$G_{j,NJ} - G_{P,NJ}(G_{j,N}/G_{P,N}) = A_j$$

where A_j could serve as a measure of the agglomeration pull on the j-th industry. However, if A_j is positive this does not necessarily indicate the presence of agglomeration economies. All that is indicated is that cost advantages exist for the industry in the area under consideration. These cost advantages could be due, for example, to reduced transfer cost as a result of gravitation to raw material sites. Thus, an industry-by-industry analysis must be conducted to determine whether or not these cost advantages are the result of agglomeration economies. In his empirical work Marcus employs the twenty two-digit manufacturing industries found in the state of New Jersey for the period 1947–62. He finds that six industries exhibited an average positive growth residual (A_j) for the entire period. Of these six industries, however, agglomeration benefits were the likely explanation in only three (printing and publishing, leather, and instruments). The specific agglomeration benefits found were argued to be related to the prominence of New York City as a fashion center; to its large supply of writing talent; and to its supply of skilled labor and entrepreneurial services.

Marcus' technique intertwines large-scale economies, urbanization economies, and localization economies, although Marcus argues that his approach reflects agglomeration due only to localization economies. The rationale for this is based upon *a priori* grounds: (1) we would not expect large-scale economies to be important in explaining agglomeration since internal scale economies could be reaped in any number of locations; and (2) urbanization economies are not important in explaining agglomeration since economies of this sort could be realized in any of a large number of urban centers (1965:279–284). It is on these grounds, as we just saw, that Hoover has criticized the work of Weber and suggested a more complete approach. A technique which separates these various agglomeration forces, as well as tests their relative contributions, rather than aggregating them together and/or dismissing several of them on *a priori* grounds, must be proposed.

Hansen (1970) suggests a similar approach. Hansen draws attention to the fact that growth in national employment has been accounted for primarily by expanding tertiary activities, which have been located for the most part in metropolitan areas. Furthermore, their growth in cities is in large measure due to external agglomeration economies. Richardson (1973a) takes Hansen's argument a stage further. Richardson argues that growth in certain service industries (e.g., banking, finance and business services) may be quite synonymous with the development of urbanization economies, while expansion in other services (e.g., entertainment and cultural amenities) may also be relevant if location decision-makers are utility rather than profit maximizers. Richardson suggests that one might be able to use growth in service industries in the widest sense (i.e., social amenities as well as business services) as a surrogate for agglomeration economies. Richardson offers two practical tests; (1) compare growth performance in all selected service industries with changes in city size; and (2) look at the interactions between changes in service and non-service industries to investigate whether agglomeration economies (as reflected in the index of service expansion) stimulate growth in other industries or not. The problem here is just how do we identify the direction of causation? Although investigations along these lines seem useful, they obviously would not represent a comprehensive list of external economies since many of the important aspects mentioned previously (e.g., labor market economies, technological externalities associated with locational agglomeration, etc.) fall outside their scope.

A somewhat different approach to the agglomeration economies measurement problem reflects the fact that many of these economies are directly related to the spatial concentration of people in metropolitan areas. Thus, population scale for cities of different sizes can be used as a proxy for agglomeration economies. The rationale for this hypothesis includes economies of scale in the provision of urban government services, in private business services, and in social, cultural and leisure facilities. Some of these can be provided more efficiently on a large scale; others can be supplied *only* above a threshold urban size because they need a large market area to support them. Likewise, the threshold analysis developed by Lösch (1938), Thompson (1965) and Pred (1966) suggests that large-scale economies tend to be positively related to population size. Also, as Clemente and Sturgis (1971) show, population size is one of the key variables determining the diversity of the economic structure of the area. Kuznets (1964) pointed to large scale economies in the use of social overhead capital and to the size of the local market

AN EMPIRICAL APPROACH

in large urban areas. Lampard (1954) emphasized advantages on the input side: the advantages of access to a metropolitan labor pool and to developed capital markets. Scale permits greater specialization and hence increased efficiency. Finally, Alonso (1971) has put forth the hypothesis that productivity of labor is positively related to urban population size.

In a similar vein, population squared has been suggested as a surrogate for agglomeration diseconomies. Support for this hypothesis is usually based upon an argument established by Baumol (1967):

> ...the logic of the argument is simple and perhaps rather general: if each inhabitant in an area imposes external costs on every other, and if the magnitude of the costs borne by each individual is roughly proportionate to population size then since these costs are borne by each of the N persons involved, the total external cost will not vary with N but with N^2.

The above hypothesis can be tested by a quadratic function:

$$A_i = a + bP_i - cP_i^2 \tag{2.1}$$

Where A_i reflects agglomeration in the i-th metropolitan area, P_i is the population in i and a, b, c are parameters.[4] Support for the hypoghesis requires that

$$b > 0 \quad \text{and} \quad c > 0$$

If c differs from zero, an optimal city size exists where

$$\frac{dA}{dP} = b - 2cP = 0$$

Solving for P

$$P' = b/2c$$

P' represents the population size at which net economies will be at a maximum. This relationship is graphically represented in fig. 2.2.

A metropolitan area of population size P' is the area in which the difference between urbanization economies and diseconomies are at a maximum. A metropolitan area with a population size less than

P' receives a positive gain from increased population size. Here net economies are increasing but at a decreasing rate. Cities beyond population size P' may be called dysfunctional urbanism, because increasing population yields net negative returns. That is, the additional diseconomies associated with metropolitan population size beyond P' overwhelm the additional external economies generated by that size.

Kawashima (1975) has employed the quadratic form to estimate optimal city size for both overall manufacturing and its corresponding two- and three-digit SIC breakdown. Kawashima employs the following relationship between value added per worker (V/L) and the capital-labor ratio (K/L), which has high explanatory power:

$$V/L = a\left(\frac{rK}{L}\right) + b$$

Where a and b are constants and r is the product rental of capital. Making the usual assumptions as to homogeneity of degree one,

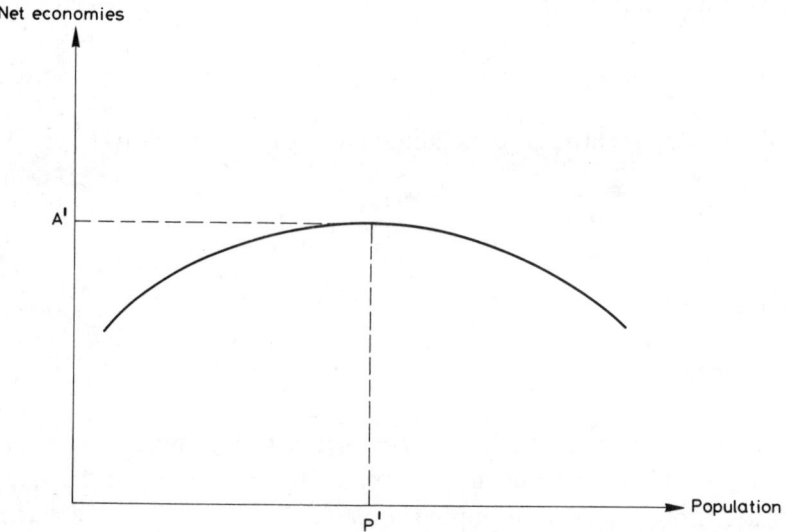

Fig. 2.2.

perfective competition in both product and factor market, etc., from the above relationship we can derive a 'labor-oriented' production function:

$$v = cK^{1/a}L^{1/a} + bL$$

In addition, if we assume that urban agglomeration economies exert an influence on the labor-oriented production function through its coefficient b (a justification for such an assumption is not attempted by Kawashima) we have the following two production functions

$$V = cK^{1/a}L^{1/a} + (d + d_1 POP) \cdot L$$
$$V = cK^{1/a}L^{1-1/a} + (d + d_2 POP - d_3 POP^2) \cdot L$$

which can be derived from the following two equations respectively:

$$\frac{V}{L} = a\left(\frac{rK}{L}\right) + d + d_1(POP)$$
$$\frac{V}{L} = a\left(\frac{rK}{L}\right) + d + d_2(POP) - d_3(POP^2)$$

d_1 represents an estimate of the index of urbanization economies and $-d_2/(2d_3)$ an estimate of the optimal city size. These estimates are presented in table 2.1 for overall manufacturing and its various two-digit subgroupings. Kawashima reports only those results which are both theoretically consistent and statistically significant. As table 2.1 indicates, urbanization economies are strong and positive for all but our very largest cities.

A similar line of reasoning has been taken up by Rasmussen (1973). Rasmussen argues that the relationship between net gains from agglomeration and city size (where population is used as a proxy for city size) may be similar to that of the total product curve commonly employed in microeconomic theory. Fig. 2.3 reproduces this curve and three stages of urban agglomeration. During stage I (OA), the gains from agglomeration are not only increasing but increasing at an increasing rate. Population increases continue to yield positive benefits during Stage II (AB), although they are now increasing, but at a decreasing rate. Stage III corresponds to 'dysfunctional' urbanism since population increases yield negative,

TABLE 2.1. Indices of urbanization economies, and optimal urban population size.

SIC industry	Index of urbanization economies	Optimal urban size (in millions)
All manufacturing		5.95
Food and kindred products	.1605	6.868
Textile mill products		
Apparel and related products	.1109	6.573
Lumber and wood products	.1117	6.502
Furniture and fixtures	.0884	6.409
Paper and allied products	.0599	5.295
Printing and publishing		
Chemicals and allied products		4.855
Petroleum and coal products	.1770	
Rubber and plastic products		4.746
Leather and leather products	0.475	5.799
Stone, clay and glass	.0841	7.124
Primary metal industries	.0561	5.058
Fabricated metal products	.0766	5.381
Machinery, except electrical	.0760	5.753
Electrical machinery	.1495	6.011
Transportation equipment	.1362	
Instruments and related products		
Miscellaneous manufacturing	.0552	5.143

Source: Kawashima (1975:167).

agglomeration effects. The optimum city size, of course, is *OB*, where net economies are greatest. Stages II and III in fig. 2.3 correspond to the relationship depicted in fig. 2.2 above.

While population grew by 13% in the U.S. between 1960 and 1970, table 2.2 shows that approximately 50% of all non-metropolitan areas actually lost population. In contrast, metropolitan areas exhibit more social and economic viability than non-metropolitan areas, as witnessed by the fact that only 15.9% of the smallest metropolitan areas lost population. Rasmussen uses maintenance of population as a criterion for economic viability, and notes that there appear to be few gains beyond 500,000. But, there appear to be significant advantages to population growth until a town achieves metropolitan status. Population size, *OA*, in fig. 2.3 indicating the beginning of Stage II, would seem to be about 50,000.

AN EMPIRICAL APPROACH

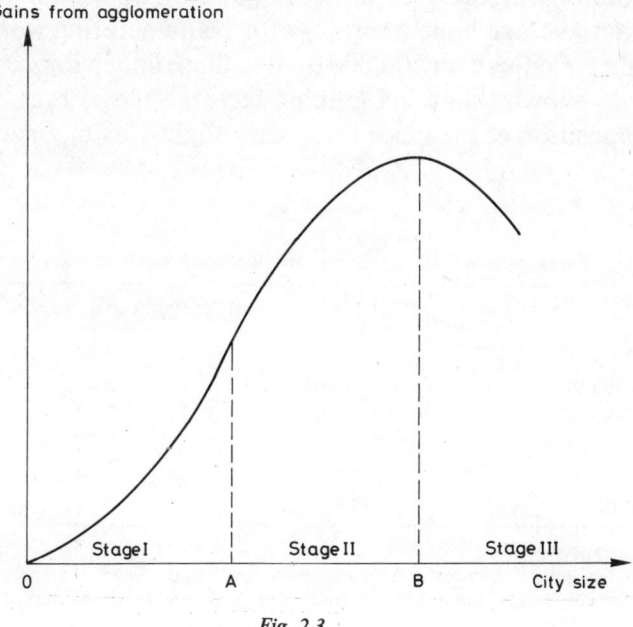

Fig. 2.3.

TABLE 2.2. Population trends in metropolitan and non-metropolitan areas, 1960–1970

Size		Areas with population losses	
	Number	Number	Percentage
1,000,000	34	1	2.9
500,000–999,999	38	1	2.6
200,000–499,999	83	6	7.2
50,000–199,999	94	15	15.9
Non-metropolitan areas*	2619	1292	49.3

Source: Rasmussen (1973:157).
*All countries outside metropolitan areas in 1970.

In Stage II the advantages of further agglomeration are reduced until the optimal city size (*OB* in fig. 2.3 which corresponds to *P'* in fig. 2.1) is reached. Alonso's hypothesis that worker productivity is a function of urban population size implies that average wages should tend to increase as urban population increases. Table 2.3 shows that average hourly earnings for manufacturing workers are 12% higher in cities over 500,000 than in those under 200,000. Fuchs (1967) has shown that demographic factors such as race, age, sex and composition of the labor force vary slightly by city size, so that

TABLE 2.3. Earnings in manufacturing for metropolitan areas in the non-South,* 1970

Size	Average hourly wage median
Under 200,000	3.34
200,000–499,999	3.57
500,000–999,999	3.74
1–2 million	3.75
2–4 million	3.83
Over 4 million	3.74

Source: Rasmussen (1973:158).
*Many studies have shown that money wages are lower in the South than elsewhere in the nation. In order to avoid any regional influence in the comparison, southern cities are omitted.

these factors which influence worker productivity are not responsible for the positive relationship between earning and city size. Based on this Rasmussen concludes that 'in the area of worker earnings, it seems there are clear economies from agglomeration until a metropolitan area reaches a population of half a million ... (or) considering both city survival and average wages, the optimum city size would seem to be a half million or larger.'[5]

Hoch (1972), however, has argued that rising wages in metropolitan areas is caused by several factors: payments for non-pecuniary disamenities (e.g., crime, congestion, etc.); and the increased living costs associated with larger metropolitan areas.

The data in tables 2.2 and 2.3, however, do not give any indication that Stage III, dysfunctional urbanism, sets in after the maximum (OB) is reached. This supports the common view held by urban economists that diseconomies rarely offset completely the economies generated by urban scale.

There are a number of serious problems with both Kawashima and Rasmussen studies. To begin with, we encounter the obstacle of just how to test Equation 2.1, the very equation both studies are founded upon, when we have no satisfactory measure of agglomeration economies to use as the dependent variable. It seems that Kawashima and Rasmussen accept the underlying hypothesis of Equation 2.1 based upon its theoretical construct, rather than offering any strong empirical evidence to support it.

Rasmussen offers us the generalization that agglomeration economies refer to the economies of size and concentration. The benefits of size and concentration, however, vary for different sectors of the urban community (e.g., for households, for society at large, for industry, as well as for different branches of industry). Therefore, it might prove more instructive to develop disaggregated techniques which discern the differences among agglomeration economies for society at large, for households and for various firms. Furthermore, Rasmussen implicitly assumes that population is homogeneous in attributes and only concentrations of population matters. Finally, Rasmussen's approach is not a statistically rigorous technique. It is based upon an analysis of the meager information given in tables 2.2 and 2.3 above.

In Kawashima's manufacturing industry and optimal city size analysis, similar problems abound. At best, population size might be reflective of the large-scale economies component. Certain population thresholds must be crossed to exploit internal scale economies. Population is not, however, very reflective of localization and urbanization economies. There is no reason to suspect a significant correlation between population and intraindustry clustering (localization economies). In addition, while population size is important for the provision of consumer or household agglomeration economies (e.g., theater, opera, professional sports, retail trade, etc.), there is little reason to believe population scale is important in the provision of business agglomeration economies found in cities (e.g., specialized business services, etc.). What this suggests is that when studying manufacturing industry, separate proxies should be utilized to break-out the various agglomeration forces—urbanization economies, localization economies, and large-scale economies – since different industries are sensitive to quite different combinations of these various forces.

Returning to the measurement problem, Harris and Wheeler (1971) and Edel (1972) have argued that agglomeration economies and diseconomies of congestion (net economies) are capitalized in land values of cities. Thus, the change in land values with city size gives some indication of the net agglomeration economies of cities of a particular size. Using a cross-sectional sample Edel finds that elasticity of land values with respect to changes in city size tends to decline as city size increases. The elasticity falls below unity between 250,000 to 500,000 declining sharply up to the million mark, but returning to above unity for metropolitan areas larger than three million. This implies that land values *per capita* peak at about 300,000 and peak again for very large cities of over three million. However, Edel argues that for these very large cities it's the corporate and hierarchial managerial functions which sustain the increase in land values. This sort of activity does not generate net social benefits but rather imposes heavy congestion costs which are incurred for the maintenance of the hierarchy while the benefits of large size are distributed regressively.

There is some merit to Edel's argument that the benefits of agglomeration accrue to the landowner, the entrepreneur, and the upper-income household while the urban poor bear a disproportionate share of the costs. It takes purchasing power to take advantage of the variety of opportunities that large cities offer. The urban poor may find themselves 'locked in' inside the urban ghetto with severely restricted choices for living and working. This argument is, however, rather limited. Edel does not explain why other groups cannot bear the fruits, as it were, of agglomeration economies. For example, why is it that the benefits of concentration do not accrue, in part at least, to entrepreneurs through higher profits as well as to workers via higher wages?

Edel's suggestion that land values may represent a measure of the net agglomeration effect is meritorious. It furthermore permits the relationship between A and P (i.e., Equation 2.1) to be tested. The analysis, however, assumes, as pointed out by Richardson (1973b), that the economic agents bidding on land can, somehow, evaluate the economies and diseconomies associated with a particular site. If, on the other hand, it is impossible for economic agents to evaluate both benefits and costs or if they underestimate them the analysis loses much of its force. Finally, both the Edel, and Harris and Wheeler studies exhibit many of the same problems as Rasmussen's work. That is, the Edel, and Harris and Wheeler approach is a much too aggregated technique for our purposes. It makes no distinction among agglomeration economies for society at large (social agglomeration economies) for households (household agglomeration economies), and for establishments (business agglomeration economies). To be sure, the optimal city size must differ for each of these groups which comprise the urban community. In addition, the optimal city size must also differ for various groups within a given sector. For example, is the optimal city size the same for establishments making up food and kindred products as for those engaged in production in the primary metal products industry? The point is that coincidence of the optimal city size for various manufacturing establishments is not likely.

A number of cluster studies have been recently undertaken. Richter (1969), Streit (1969), Struyk (1972), Latham (1976), Bopp and Gordon (1977) and Tybout and Mattila (1977) have studied clustering in manufacturing, without considering interaction with service and tertiary activities. Stanback and Knight (1970) have described how employment shares in highly aggregated sectors vary with city size, and how some of these sectors exhibit common locational patterns. Finally, Bergsman, Greenston and Healy (1972), have extended the work of these cluster studies by focusing on: (1) techniques for identifying industrial clusters; (2) the relation of economic structure to growth rate of metropolitan areas; and (3) the role of non-manufacturing industries in producing agglomeration.

In concluding this survey, we will now take up various production function approaches to the measurement problem. Since production function analysis is employed in the empirical chapter of this work, a critical examination of such previous applications is now in order.

Kawashima's production function approach has already been introduced and critically examined. A somewhat different production function application has been suggested by Rocca (1970), Sveikauskas (1975), and Segal (1976). All three papers suggest a production function of the following generalized form

$$q = g(A) \cdot f(X_1, X_2)$$

which relates output, q, to the amount of factors X_1 and X_2, employed and to the amount of all other factors linked to the total volume of production and represented by $g(A)$. Insofar as $g(A)$ stands for the net effect of external economies and diseconomies, and assuming that

$$\partial q/\partial g(A) \cdot \partial g(A)/\partial A > 0$$

one can imagine a family of production functions, each of which are at a higher level, the higher the value of $g(A)$. Rocca, Sveikauskas, and Segal assume that the production function characterizing the unit under consideration is identical across cities (i.e., they employ cross-sectional analysis), while differences from city-to-city due to natural endowments, proximity to other cities, infrastructure, and so on, are captured by the constant term. Sveikauskas and Segal go one step further and argue that size itself can be thought of as a site characteristic, imbedded in the constant term of the production function. The essential question becomes whether the impact of size (measured by city population scale) is positive, negative or neutral across the size distribution of cities. The *a priori* hypothesis is that size exerts a positive influence on city productivity.

The empirical findings of both the Sveikauskas and Segal studies indicate that size is positive and significant for the units under consideration. However, both studies are subject to serious qualifications. To begin with, the assumption that production structures are identical across cities seems unlikely. More troublesome, however, is the level of aggregation employed. Segal's analysis is at the SMSA level, which raises, once again, the usual question as to how size influences different groups comprising the urban environment (e.g., how does urban population size affect social, household, and business agglomeration economies?) Sveikauskas' analysis, on the other hand, is at the two-digit SIC code manufacturing industry breakdown. This is somewhat more useful in that it tells us something, if the hypothesis is correct, about *average* productivity of large cities. It does not reveal anything about the productivity of particular cities or region of the country.

Moreover, both productivity and city size are caused by another factor, namely, external economies. The extent of these external economies depends upon the number of activities within a city and not on it's population size.

Finally, and most important for our purposes, is that this sort of production function approach sheds no new light on the measurement question. A more direct attempt at measuring the agglomeration variable has been suggested by Shefer (1973). Shefer employs two variants of the CES production function, in which data for the capital stock were not required to estimate returns to scale parameters. The objective of the paper was the measurement of localization economies in two-digit manufacturing industries in the U.S. for two independent time periods – 1958–1963 using cross-sectional data. Shefer found localization economies do prevail in the two-digit manufacturing industries and that his conclusion can be drawn for both models used. Although his results were interesting, the scale parameters were quite unstable over the five-year period. In addition, there exists a considerable amount of variation between the estimates obtained from the two models. Census of manufacture data were employed to conduct an industry-by-industry cross-sectional analysis. There are, however, a number of extreme problems with cross-sectional production function applications. The increasing returns to scale parameter is estimated under the assumption that both technology and factor prices are identical across cities. As suggested above, the assumption that technology is identical across cities is questionable. There is evidence which indicates that the spatial diffusion of innovation begins in the largest urban places and then tends to be transmitted down along the hierarchy of cities. If this is so, at any given point in time similar establishments located in cities of different sizes will be employing not identical but different levels of technology.

Moreover, the long-run average cost curve is drawn on the assumption of identical factor prices for similar establishments across cities. But to the extent that factor prices vary across cities and assuming that the least-cost combination of inputs is sought, the particular "mix" chosen at any level of scale depends *inter alia* on input price ratios. Thus a long-run average cost curve applicable to an industry in a particular city, with a given set of factor prices, must be different from the long-run average cost curve of that same industry located in a different city, with a different set of factor prices. Cross-sectional production function techniques which attempt to estimate returns to scale for a given industry across cities are therefore misapplied.

Even if we could assume identical technology and factor prices across cities, problems for regional analysis still exists. By estimating returns to scale on a cross-sectional industry-by-industry basis, everything about distinctions of place is lost. What we end up with is an average scale coefficient for the industry under consideration across all SMSA's. All that this tells us is that on average total scale economies for the various industries exist. In the next chapter, we will discuss how to employ one of these techniques to estimate total scale economies for an average establishment in a given SMSA, using time-series data. Time-series application enables much of the distinctions of place to be maintained. In addition, these estimates of total scale economies can in turn be employed as dependent variables in an industry-by-industry cross-sectional regression model designed to analyze the contribution contributed to total scale by large-scale economies, localization economies, urbanization economies, and urbanization diseconomies. Supplying details about the time-series and cross-sectional models is the purpose of the next chapter.

2.4. CONCLUSION

In this chapter, we explored both the theoretical development, as well as some of the suggested measurement techniques, with respect to agglomeration economies. While agglomeration economies are well defined in the urban/regional literature, they have not been adequately measured. As we saw, most of the measures proposed are, at best, highly aggregated (e.g., Rasmussen and Edel's techniques). Indeed, it is precisely the measurement problem which led Richardson to comment: 'The main problems arise when we attempt to measure these economies (agglomeration economies) precisely enough for use in an operational model. The failure to break this bottleneck satisfactorily remains possibly the most serious obstacle to progress in applied regional economics.'[6] It is this observation which gave impetus to the present study. The existing work, both theoretical and empirical, will prove useful to us in the next chapter where we discuss the rationale upon which our empirical approach to measuring and disaggregating the agglomeration variable for U.S. manufacturing establishments is based.

NOTES

1. Hoover (1937:90–91) notes that his classification of agglomeration forces had previously been suggested in the works of Ohlin (1967) and Robinson (1962). Robinson divides external economies into mobile and immobile economies. Mobile economies are those external economies not dependent on the size of the industry in a particular location, but rather on its size in the entire country or the world as a whole, whereas immobile economies include other external economies available only to the firms concentrated in a particular area.
2. Vernon (1960) provides evidence which suggests that most agglomeration economies are more relevant for locational decisions made by small firms than for large firms especially since the latter can internalize many of them.
3. Empirical analysis of the spatial diffusion process has been developed in geography. See Hagerstrand (1952, 1966, and 1967). The contribution made by economists in this area has been conducted by Griliches (1957) and Mansfield (1968).
4. A similar functional form was employed by Williamson and Swanson (1966) and Garofalo (1974) to test the proposition that the urban growth function might have an inverted U-shape taking the form

   $$g = a + b_1 P - b_2 P^2$$

   where g is the growth rate, however measured.
5. Rasmussen (1973:157).
6. Richardson (1973a:157).

3. Agglomeration and location of manufacturing activity: the theoretical framework

3.1. INTRODUCTION

The primary purpose of this chapter is to articulate the theoretical framework upon which the empirical analysis, in the next chapter, will be conducted. The view put forth is that indivisibilities in production are the main forces leading to scale economies in the widest sense, and agglomeration of manufacturing activity. Since production function analysis is a technique consistent with this theoretical scheme, a variant of the CES production function is proposed to measure scale economies. A two-fold approach will be employed: (1) time-series analysis will be utilized to estimate agglomeration or scale coefficients directly for each two-digit SIC industry in a given SMSA via production function techniques; (2) these scale coefficients will then be employed as a dependent variable in a cross-sectional industry-by-industry regression model designed to decompose the agglomeration measure into: (a) internal scale economies; (b) localization economies; (c) urbanization economies; and (d) urbanization diseconomies.

3.2. CENTRAL PLACE THEORY AND AGGLOMERATION

Economic activity in general, and manufacturing establishments in particular, are not spread evenly and in a continuous fashion over space. With the exception of activities such as agriculture, forestry and fishery, production is concentrated in comparatively few centers or agglomerations. These concentrations of manufacturing activity are not of the same size, nor do they have identical or similar economic structure. Centers of different size are not the locations of the same industries, rather, there are systematic differences in the industrial structure of centers according to size. This situation is related to another feature of the spatial structure, the fact that in some industries production is carried on in few production units

CENTRAL PLACE THEORY AND AGGLOMERATION

only, while in other industries production is distributed over a large number of plants spread over many centers, or clustered in a few large centers. One theory which highlights the basic factors giving rise to spatial patterns of concentrations is central place analysis of Christaller (1966) and Lösch (1954).

In their theoretical systems both Lösch and Christaller made the following assumptions: (1) an isotropic surface, i.e., transportation cost is equal in all directions from any point on the surface; (2) a homogeneous plain with a uniform rural population; (3) a system of f.o.b. pricing (i.e., the consumer pays the price at the point of production plus the cost of transportation to the consumer's location); (4) each consumer has identical tastes and income; (5) an individual develops no preferences for patronizing any given center over any other center, except that he will always patronize the nearest center offering a given level of the service; (6) only ubiquitous inputs are used to produce any output. That is, highly localized inputs such as iron ore or cooking coal do not enter into any production activities; and (7) that there are no institutional or legal restrictions on the entry of producers into the market.

The point of departure in Lösch's analysis was the conventional downward-sloping individual demand curve. Given the foregoing assumptions, the quantity of output demanded by an individual consumer depends on the price of the product at the plant and the distance of the consumer from the plant. An individual demand curve is shown in fig. 3.1. If the price at the plant were OP, the consumers adjacent to the plant would purchase PP' units. At a distance from P, price will be higher than OP by the amount of freight and consequently demand will fall. At the distance where freight costs are equal to PY, no units of output will be sold. Thus PY represent the extreme sales radius of the plant.

The total quantity demanded from the producer at price OP is equal to the volume of the demand cone obtained from rotating $PP'Y$ on PP' as the vertical axis times the population density (fig. 3.2).

There is a different demand cone for each price set at the plant. For example, if the price at the plant were less than OP, more units would be demanded by consumers adjacent to the plant. In addition, demand would vanish farther from the plant. Thus, the height and base of the cone would be larger, as well as the volume. This result can be drawn as a new curve, DD in fig. 3.3, which gives total

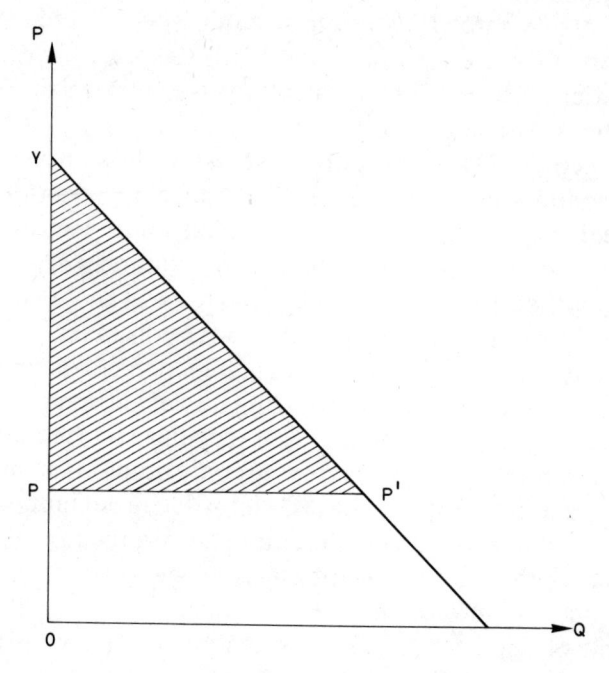

Fig. 3.1

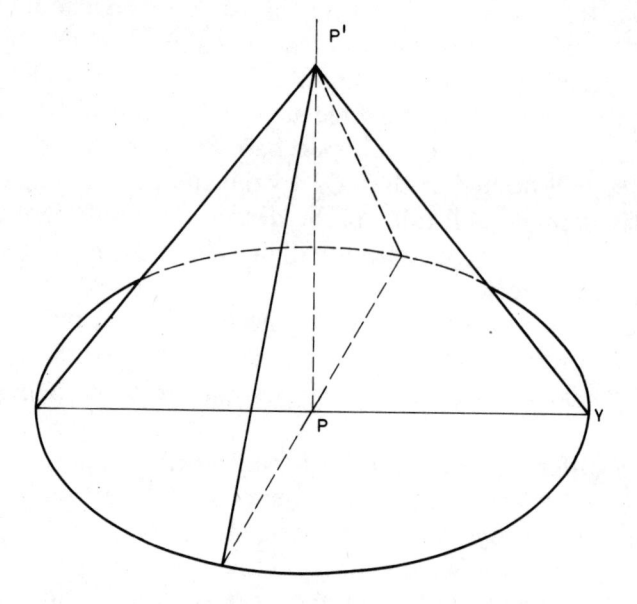

Fig. 3.2

demand as a function of f.o.b. price.[1] Also shown in fig. 3.3 is the average cost curve (*AC*) which represents the cost of production per unit of output. It is assumed that a 'normal profit' is included as part of the overall production cost. The intersection of marginal cost and marginal revenue curves determines the profit-maximizing price OP_1 and the profit-maximizing output OQ_2.

The demand curve *DD* has been constructed under the assumption that market areas are circular. Such a shape ensures that the largest possible area is contained within a given distance of the plant. But circular market areas leave interstitial areas which are not served by any plant (fig. 3.4a), whereas the assumptions require that all areas of the plain be served. In addition, all establishments must have the same size and shape of market area. There exist only three regular geometric figures which fulfill these requirements – hexagons, squares, and equilateral triangles. Lösch demonstrates that in market regions of a given area, the total demand in a hexagon is 2.4% greater than in a square and 12% greater than in an equilateral triangle (1954:111–113). Thus, the hexagon is the most effi-

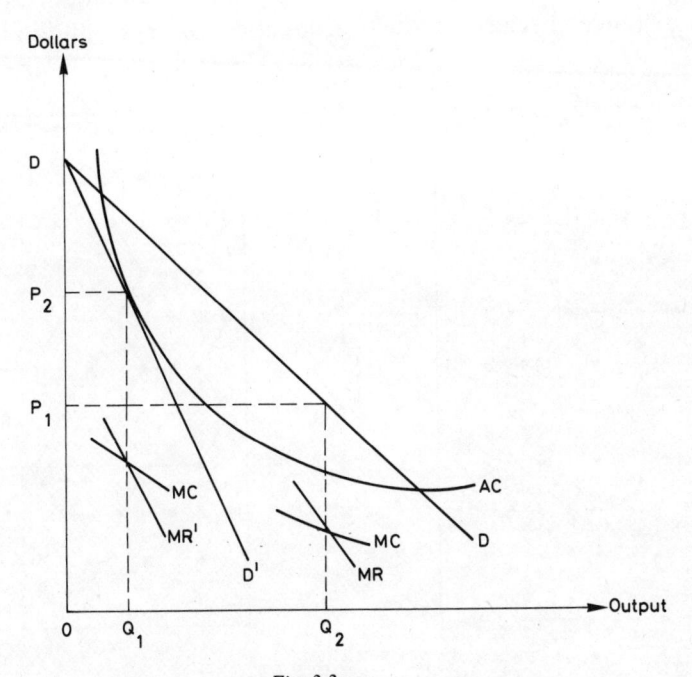

Fig. 3.3.

cient shape for a firm's market area (fig. 3.4b). Just as the shape of the market is changed from circular to hexagonal, so must the market area that any plant commands be reduced by competition from other establishments until only normal profits are made by all plants. This thereby diminishes a plant's demand curve from DD to DD', which is just tangent to AC in fig. 3.3. The plant is then at its minimum profitable size, producing OQ_1 units of output, and the market is full.[2]

Next, Lösch examines the spacing of settlements. One plant, in the Löschian framework, can serve 2, 3, 4, 7, 9, 12, 13, 16, 19, 21, 25, ... settlements, the number depending upon economies of scale (declining average cost) and transport costs within the industry (1954:116–122).

Finally, hexagonal nets are derived in this fashion for each industry. Lösch proceeds then to lay the nets together 'so that *all* of them have at least one center in common. Here a metropolis will arise, with all the advantages of a large local demand. Second, we turn the nets about this center in such a way as to get six sectors with many and six with only a few production sites (fig. 3.5). With this arrangement the greatest number of locations coincide, the maximum distances between industrial locations is least, and in conse-

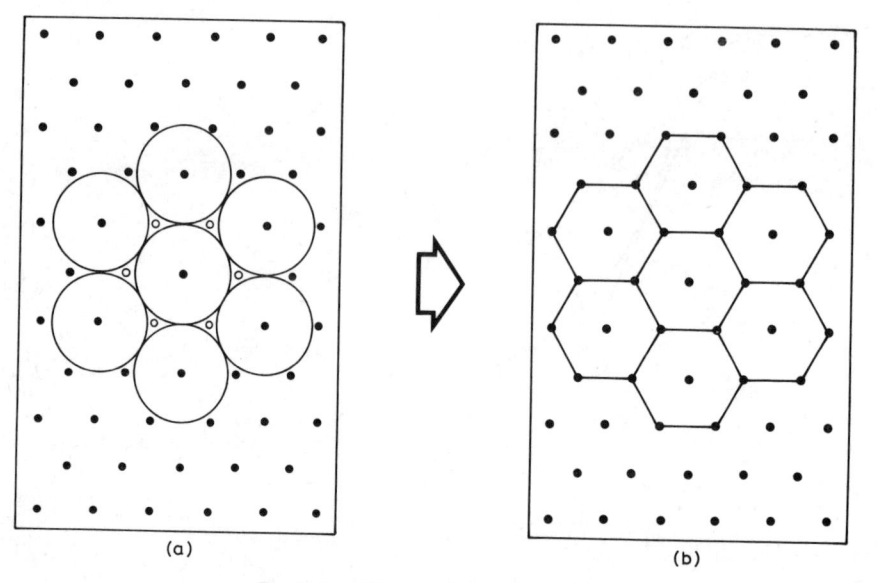

Fig. 3.4a,b. (Source: Isard 1975:314).

quence not only shipments but also transport lines are reduced to a minimum' (1954:124)

In summary, the main features of this system may now be gathered. The production and selling points for every good are regular-

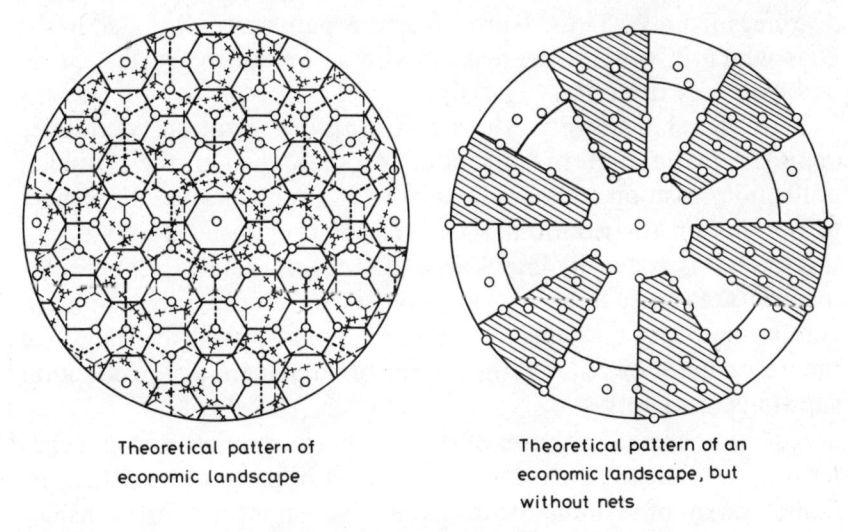

Theoretical pattern of
economic landscape

Theoretical pattern of an
economic landscape, but
without nets

Fig. 3.5. (Source: Lösch: 1954:125).

ly distributed over the plain, each point having a hexagonal market area the size of which depends on transport costs and economies of scale internal to the plant. Selling points of different goods tend to agglomerate, technically because of the rotation of nets, and economically because of agglomeration forces which operate to minimize transport costs and to maximize local demand (i.e., urbanization economies in our terms). There exist in Lösch's framework many of these agglomerations (central places), but their number diminishes as the number of functions within them increases; consequently the spacing of higher order centers is wider than that of lower order central places.

A good summary of the criticisms of central place theory is given by Greenhut (1956), Isard (1956:48; 270–274), and Paelinck and Nijkamp (1975:70). Several of these criticisms are relevant to the present study. Isard, for example, has pointed out an inconsistency in the Löschian analysis. Lösch's construct yields different sizes of concentrations of industrial activity. Such concentration of activities, however, implies a concentration of jobs and thus households, thereby contradicting the initial assumption of uniform distribution of population. Due to this larger concentration of population at the core, the size of a market area necessary to generate sufficient demand for a community is much smaller at the core than at greater distances from it. Thus, Isard obtains a pattern of distorted hexagons which in general decrease in size as we approach the central city from any direction (fig. 3.6).

Thus fig. 3.6 suggests the impact of urbanization economies upon the spatial patterns of production sites when all the Löschian uniformity assumptions hold, except for modification with respect to population distribution. As Lösch (1938) himself points out in this case, it is generally impossible to arrange a set of irregular nets over an area in such a way that they all have at least one point in common: no city contains a complete set of all industries, and since the nets cannot be rotated the degree of coincidence of production sites falls markedly.

A second basic limitation of the Löschian argument is that it cannot account for localization economies. Lösch presented the view that a system of rational locations requires an intraindustry dispersion of plants and an interindustry concentration of establishments. One reason that intraindustry (localization) economies do not arise is due to the assumption that raw materials are ubiquitous and everywhere available at the same costs. Thus, intraindustry gravitation to a raw material site is ruled out. Furthermore, central place theory cannot handle economies internalized within the industry brought about by spatial juxtaposition, i.e., the type of agglomeration which Weber treated extensively.

Greenhut (1956:269–272) has argued, however, that the Löschian framework can be modified to account for localization economies under conditions of locational interdependence and uncertainty. Greenhut suggests that there are interdependence factors which would give rise to intraindustry concentration even in a situation characterized by even distribution of resources. The profit motive alone causes uncertainty with respect to the location policies of competing firms, which tends to promote concentration of an industry.

Moreover, even in the absence of locational interdependence, the existence of (1) unequal costs at alternative locations, due, if for no other reason, to agglomeration advantages; (2) a demand curve

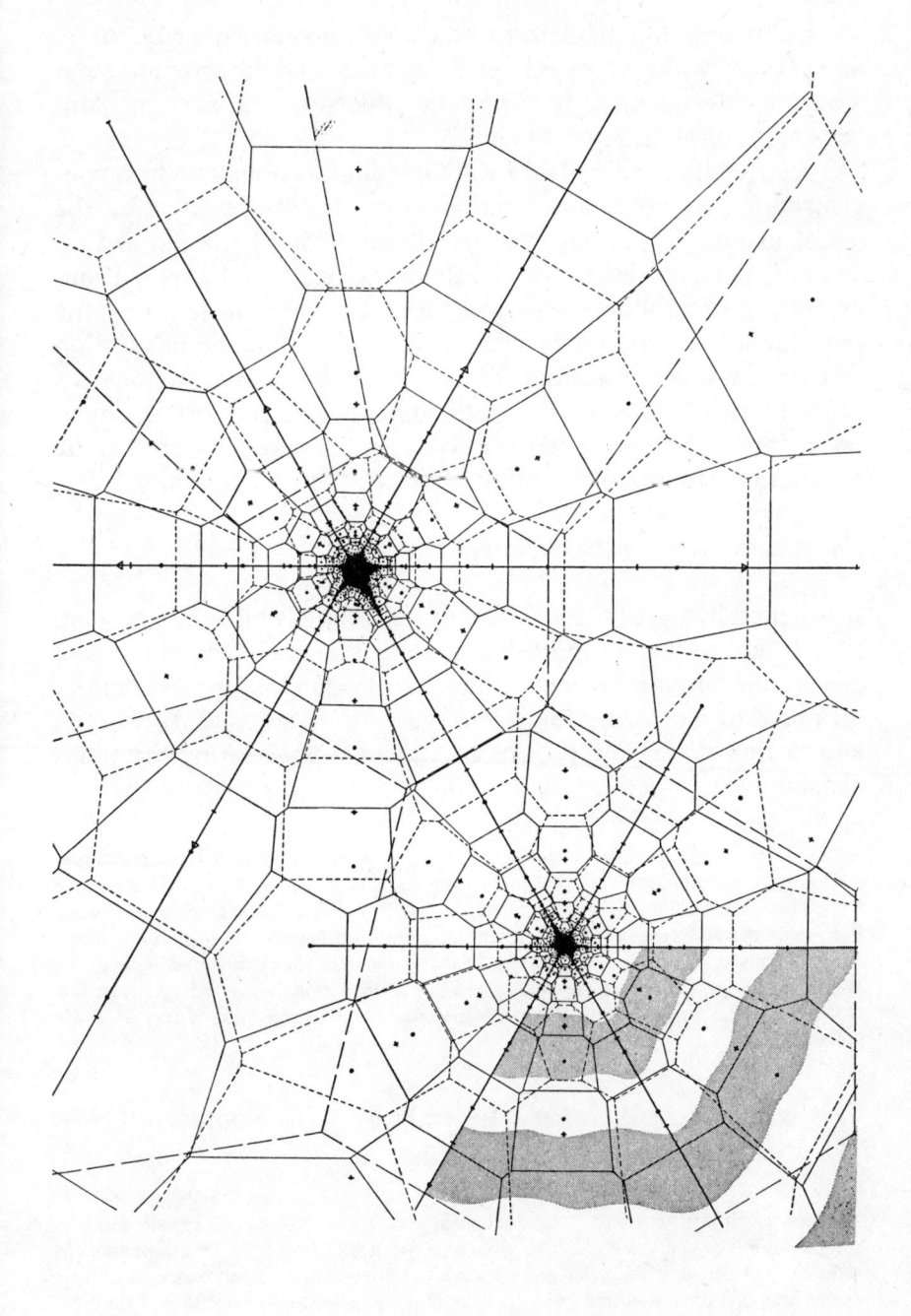

Fig. 3.6. (Source: W. Isard 1956:272).

approximating infinite inelasticity; (3) a rising marginal cost curve; and (4) a very low ratio between freight rate and the price intercept would create uncertainty regarding dispersion and promote concentration of an industry (1956:270).

These points rised by Isard and Greenhut demonstrate how concentrations of population and industry results, even given the initial assumption about even distributions of population and resources. For any theory which attempts to explain the spatial concentration of production in comparatively few central places the introduction of indivisible factors of production or production processes becomes essential. These indivisibilities or advantages associated with large-scale activities do not permit proportionality to be maintained at all levels of production among all inputs in the production process, and lead to increasing returns to scale.

3.3. THE THEORETICAL FRAMEWORK

It is generally agreed by economists that indivisibilities in production do not permit proportionality to be maintained at all levels of production among all inputs into the production process, and in turn lead to increasing returns to scale. Nicholas Kaldor (1934:65) argues that increasing returns to scale are necessarily due to indivisibilities:

> ... it appears methodologically convenient to treat all cases of large-scale economies under the heading 'indivisibility'. This introduces a certain unity into analysis and makes possible at the same time a clarification of the relationship between the different kinds of economies. Even the cases of increasing returns where a more-than-proportionate increase in output occurs merely on account of an increase in the amounts of the factors used, without any change in the proportions of the factors, are due to indivisibilities; only in this case it is not so much the 'original factors', but the specialized functions of those factors which are indivisible.

This was stated somewhat differently by T. C. Koopmans (1957: 151–152):

> The relevant aspect of worker specialization appears to be that, up to a certain degree of specialization, the undivided attention given by a specialized worker to a full-time task of a sufficiently challenging character produces not exactly (but presumably more than) twice as much as half-time attention (with half the training) given to the same task, if the other half of the worker's time (and training) is applied to a different productive activity.
> Similarly, many pieces of capital equipment have the characteristic that the ratios of

inputs into their manufacture to outputs from their use cannot be reproduced at a smaller scale. In both cases there is a commodity, labor or equipment, with which one cannot realistically associate a parameter expressing its amount, in such a way that this amount can be reduced below a natural unit without qualitative change, that is, without change in the ratios of inputs to output in at least one of the processes in which it is made or used.

From the production function point of view increasing returns to scale imply that an increase of all inputs in the same proportion leads to a more than proportional increase in the output. In terms of the cost function increasing returns to scale lead to decreasing production costs per unit of product as production levels go up, up to some point. Consider fig. 3.7 where a long-run average cost curve

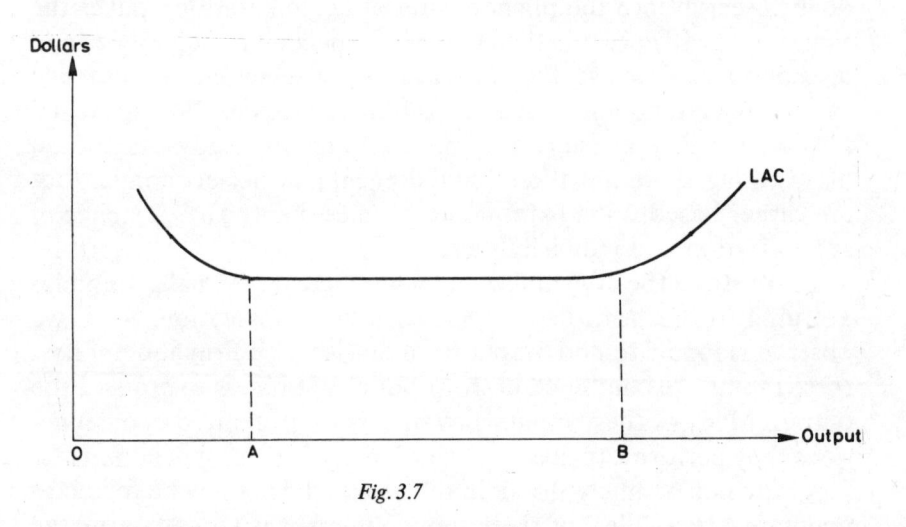

Fig. 3.7

(LAC) is represented. In fig. 3.7 we have increasing returns to scale or decreasing LAC up to output OA; constant returns to scale or constant LAC between the output levels OA and OB; past output OB, decreasing returns to scale or increasing LAC sets in.

The long-run cost function may be formally derived from the production function if the latter is known. A direct derivation, however, can become messy business even for very simple production functions. Ferguson (1969:163–168) has demonstrated this derivation for the Cobb-Douglas and CES forms.

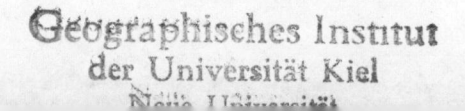

So far we have been discussing economies of scale internal to the firm consequent upon the enlargement of the firm's scale of production at one point. Indeed, internal economies of scale are a major force leading to the concentration of production in production units instead of production being spread continuously over the plane of location possibilities.

As we saw in the survey chapter of this work, internal economies are only one of several sources leading to concentration or agglomeration of production. Technological external economies also enter the production function and are an essential ingredient for any explanation of industrial conglomeration. In the survey chapter, no distinction was drawn between pecuniary and technological economies. Apparently, location theorists have not found such a distinction necessarily useful. Latham (1976:12), who has also done research into the phenomenon of agglomeration, makes the same point. It is our belief, that while pecuniary economies and diseconomies do exist, they are, at best, of secondary importance to an understanding of agglomeration economies. The principal phenomena giving rise to external agglomeration advantages and disadvantages are not these limited pecuniary net economies, but are rather based upon external economies due to the existence of specialization and indivisibilities.

To illustrate the advantages of technological external economies accruing to the firm, let us consider a firm in isolation. What we observe is inputs to and output from our isolated firm and not how these inputs are combined in the productive process to produce the output. Many of these inputs may be highly specialized in the functions they perform. In addition, since many of these specialized factors may not be finely divisible our isolated firm may be forced to maintain 'stock-piles' of these inputs unless it is willing to run the risk of delay when these inputs are required. For example, our hypothetical isolated firm may be forced to employ maintenance personnel specialized in the replacement and repair of machinery used in the factory on a full-time basis, when, in fact, this personnel is only required part of the time. Other examples of this sort might include: specialized accounting and legal personnel; large inventories of intermediate inputs; a stock of labor with specialized skill and training of the type our isolated firm needs, etc. When we take our hypothetical firm out of isolation, however, external economies soon develop. The nature of these external economies is that they permit a *reduction* in the 'stock-pile' of specialized inputs the firm needs on hand per unit of time. An extended discussion of how these reductions are occasioned shall now be taken up.

3.3.1 Internal scale economies

In each industry with given technology and factor costs there is an optimum size of plant. It is the plant which, if operated at full capacity, would give the lowest average cost of production.

The optimum size may be considered as the result of four sets of factors – technical, managerial, marketing and finance. As pointed out by Robinson (1962) and Guthrie (1955) minimum average cost for each function may occur at rates of production different from each other. Thus, a large firm may be able to reduce average costs by the manner in which it combines the scale of operation of each factor. When a plant is not at the optimum from all four standpoints, there may be a difference between the optimum-size plant and optimum-size firm.

As the size of plant and the scale of operation become larger certain economies of scale are usually realized, up to some point. One primary reason for this is specialization and the division of labor. Proficiency is gained by concentration of effort. If a plant is small and employs few workers, each worker will usually have to perform several different jobs in the productive process. In so doing he is likely to have to move about the plant, change tools, etc. Thus important savings may be realized by expanding the scale of operation. A larger plant with a larger work force may permit each worker to narrowly specialize, gaining proficiency and eliminating time consuming interchanges of location and equipment.

Another sort of technological economy that could become important is that if several different machines, each with a different rate of output, are required in a production process, the operation may have to be quite large to permit proper 'meshing' of machinery. Another example of the technological economies is the fact that the cost of purchasing and installing larger machines is usually proportionately less than the cost of smaller machines. Still another example is that as the scale of operation expands there is usually a qualitative, as well as quantitative, change in equipment. That is, expansion of scale normally permits the introduction of various types of automation devices, all of which tend to reduce per unit cost of production.

As the scale of plant expands beyond a certain point, however, diseconomies of scale may set in. For example, the efficiency in use of factors of production could decline as the quantity of the factors used by a plant increases. Here the effectiveness of management may decline as scale is increased. This may result because as the chain of management is extended delays occur in making decisions. Also, there is a tendency for those ultimately making decisions to get out of touch with events affecting the decisions brought about by the length of the management chain. Turning to labor relations, as scale is increased, people may just simply work less well. As the length of production runs increase this may result in specialized and/or repetitive work which results in worker alienation. An example of worker alienation has been reported for the auto industry by Edwards, Reich, and Weisskopf (1972:258):

Some assembly-line workers are so turned off, managers report with astonishment, that they just walk away in mid-shift and don't even come back to get their pay for time they have worked...

In some plants worker discontent has reached such a degree that there has been overt sabotage. Screws have been left in brake drums, tool handles welded into fender compartments (to cause mysterious, unfindable, and eternal rattles), paint scratched, and upholstery cut.

3.3.2. Localization economies

As the number of establishments in an industry increases in a given location, economies external to the firm but internal to its industry may become important, the spatial concentration of an industry permits the development of 'common pools' of highly specialized factors of production which are shared by many firms in the industry. The development of these 'common pools' thereby enables any particular firm in the industry to reduce the level of inventories of these factors on hand per unit time. For example, in isolation any firm might have to have on hand maintenance crews, and related equipment and spare parts to minimize down-time. The plant must, however, employ these factors on a full-time basis even though their services enter into the productive process quite infrequently. But, with the development of the industry in a common area, firms specializing in the replacement and repair of the machinery used in the industry develop, which supply services to many firms in the industry. Other examples of this sort include: the development of a firm's suppliers providing speedy replacement of suddenly depleted inventories, which affords entrepreneurs the opportunity of maintaining smaller amounts of stock on hand; the development and better organization of labor and raw material markets with respect to the availability of laborers and materials when needed by any particular plant, thereby reducing the 'stock-piles' of these factors required on hand; and specialized brokers, legal and technical personnel which develop, and once again, occasion a reduction in the 'stock-piles' of these factors firms need on hand.

Furthermore, economies of scale are sometimes secured by having firms which specialize narrowly in the making of one or several intermediate inputs used by other firms in the industry. A classic example of vertical complexes of this sort is the concentration of the garment industry in New York. The concentration of the garment industry in New York has permitted the specialization of firms within the industry, e.g., buttonhole and zipper manufacturers. If each firm in this industry had to produce its own buttonholes and zippers, production costs would increase since no single firms could generate enough output to develop economies in zipper and buttonhole making. By concentrating in a single area, however, firms specializing in these activities can develop economies of scale since they can provide these services for many firms in the garment industry (Lichtenberg, 1960).

Finally, intraindustry concentration results in a reduction in transport inputs used to bring inputs to and/or ship output from the point of production.

3.3.3. Urbanization economies

Urbanization economies permit a firm to reduce the 'stock-piles' of factors it needs to maintain per unit of time as a result of increases in the total economic size at a given location. Examples of urbanization economies are quite similar to those used to illustrate localization economies, except now they apply to all industries. They include, for example, the development of and access to large and varied labour pools; the existence of entrepreneurial talent; and the presence of wholesaling facilities in urban areas which reduces the level of inventories firms need on hand. In addition, economies of scale can also be secured by firms which specialize narrowly in the making of one or more intermediate inputs or services used by other firms in many industries. Examples here include the existence of commercial, financial and banking services and specialized business services (e.g., computer services, advertising agencies, accounting and legal facilities and R and D agencies). Moreover, interindustry juxtaposition occasions a reduction in transport inputs required to bring inputs to as well as ship output from the production site.

There are, of course, limits to the advantages associated with external economies. As cities grow large certain diseconomies develop. Mills (1972b) has argued that land and transportation resources are inputs into most productive processes. If some land is more productive than other land (e.g., near water which can be used for cooling or transportation) it will pay to concentrate production on better land. However, the limited availability of desirable land will show up as a diseconomy of scale as the amount of land used increases by forcing resort to less and less productive land. Likewise, as population size increases this could entail diseconomies in the use of transportation resources. What the Mill's hypothesis implies is that as city population size increases the boundary of the urban area is pushed further out thereby requiring more transportation resources used by the firm since inputs going into as well as output from the point of production make longer trips.

3.4. THE TECHNIQUE OF MEASURING AGGLOMERATION FORCES: THE MODEL

In the preceeding section indivisibilies were viewed as the major force leading to economies of scale in production and concentration of manufacturing activity in comparatively few urbanized centers. In this section we will attempt to construct a technique for measuring economies of scale for the various two-digit standard industrial classification industries in the United States. For this purpose production function analysis employing time series data for a given industrial establishment in a particular SMSA is appropriate.

Traditionally, economies of scale were viewed as a reduction in the long run average cost curve. Alternatively, and in accordance with the theory outlined, economies of scale can be investigated from the production function side, a production function is a mathematical expression showing the maximum amount of output which can be produced from any specific set of inputs, given the existing technology:

$$Y_i = G(X_{1i}, X_{2i}, \ldots, X_{ni})$$

THE TECHNIQUE OF MEASURING AGGLOMERATION FORCES

Where Y_i represents the output of the i-th firm measured in physical units of product, and $X_{1i}, \ldots, X_{ni}$ are the inputs of the n factors of production used by firm i, also measured in physical units.

To simplify the analysis two factors of production, capital (k) and labor (l) are usually assumed:

$$q_i = f(k_i, l_i)$$

The concept of a production function can be applied to the economy as whole, a region of the country, a metropolitan area, an entire industry, etc. Thus, for an aggregate industry production function we can write:

$$Q = F(K, L)$$

where

$$Q = \sum_i q_i, \, K = \sum_i k_i \text{ and } L = \sum_i l_i$$

There are several pitfalls associated with the application of aggregate production function analysis. Strictly speaking, a production function is a relationship between physical output of a product and the physical inputs of various factors of production which are used to produce it. However, in most production function studies output is represented not in physical but in value terms, and inputs of labor and capital are represented by man-hours of labor employed and by an estimate of the dollar value of the capital stock. This raises a serious difficulty. Consider the case of labor; labor of a different type and skill should be treated as a separate input; whereas we now treat all labor as homogeneous and capable of being measured simply in man-hours. There could be important changes in labour input resulting from changes in the skill, geographical location, and occupational composition of the labor force which would not be reflected in our homogenous labor. Joan Robinson raised a similar criticism of measuring the capital stock, which incidentally ignited the now famous Cambridge Capital Controversary:

He (the student of economics) is instructed to assume all workers alike, and to measure L in man-hours of labor; he is told something about the index-number problem involved in choosing a unit of output; and then he is hurried on to the next question, in the hope that he will forget to ask in what units C (capital) is measured. Before ever he does ask, he has become a professor, and so sloppy habits of thought are handed on from one generation to the next.[3]

Thus, when undertaking an industrial study, for example, we assume implicitly that each establishment produces a homogeneous product and uses homogeneous factor inputs. These assumptions have hardly been met by any industrial groupings in the U.S. which represent more often than not a wide range of products, each with its own unique type of input requirement. This problem will be considered at some length in the next chapter.

3.4.1. Technical change

Thus far we have operated under the tacit assumption that a production function is unchanging over the period of analysis; our case has been strictly static. Technical knowledge can be defined as the set of production processes known at a certain moment of time. Technical progress is the variation of this technical horizon. In a paper written in 1957, Solow attempted to disentangle the sources of economic growth in the United States during the period 1909–1949, using a model in which all technological change was assumed to be of the neutral-disembodied variety, i.e., progress that consists of organizational improvements which increases output given the same level of inputs over time. In addition, he assumed constant returns to scale and that factors of production are paid the value of their marginal physical products, i.e., perfect competition. In this case the production function may be written

$$Q_t = A_t F(K_t, L_t)$$

Where $F(K_t, L_t)$ is the constant-returns production function and A_t is a *steady* autonomous upward shift in the production function, i.e.,

$$A_t = A_0 e^{rt}$$

Where A_0 and r are constants, t represents time, and e is the base of natural logarithm. It can be easily shown that r represents the rate at which the production function shifts-up over time.

Technical progress need not be neutral, i.e., raises the marginal products of labour and capital in the same proportion. Technical progress could be either capital-saving or labor saving. Technical progress is said to be capital-saving (labor-saving) if it raises the marginal product of labor (capital) relative to the marginal product of capital (labor). However, a more important question is whether technological change is embodied in labor or capital.

Both Solow (1962) and Nelson (1964) have developed simple models which embody technical progress in the capital stock through the assumption that new machines are more efficient than old ones. Both assume that capital goods produced in any year are k percent more productive than capital goods produced the year before. Thus, an increase in investment reduces the average age of the capital stock, giving an increase in the rate of technical progress, which, in turn, increases the rate of growth of output beyond the increase associated with a simple increase in the number of machines available. That is, provided that investment is sufficient to reduce the average age of the capital stock, the rate of growth of output will rise both because there is more capital, and because the average machine is becoming younger. However, once the capital stock reaches its equilibrium average age for a given ratio of investment to output, this additional 'push' to output growth from capital growth will vanish, and the growth rate of output will settle into its long-run value.

L. C. Thurow and L. D. Taylor (1966) consider the possibility that technical change is partly embodied and partly disembodied. In addition, they allow for the embodiment of technical progress in labor as well as in capital. Here it is assumed that the quality of the labor force increases from year to year as a result of increased education, improved health, etc.

While the research we have just briefly outlined is ingenious and a study of it brings out some of the difficulties in isolating the factors responsible for growth, the empirical results are inconclusive and somewhat discouraging. Studies of this sort have thus far proved incapable of telling us whether technology is primarily embodied or disembodied or of giving us an idea of how strong an impact a change in the rate of investment is likely to have in changing the growth rate. Furthermore, most studies assume constant returns to scale rather than trying to disentangle the contribution of scale economies. In sum, while the problem of growth has been well delineated it is, in the main, unsolved.

3.4.2. Returns to scale

Returns to scale are easily defined for homogeneous production functions. Assuming three factors of production – capital (K), labor (L) and transportation inputs (T). A production function is homogeneous of degree h in these inputs if

$$f(tK, tL, tT) = t^h f(K, L, T)$$

Assuming, for simplicity, a Cobb-Douglas form

$$Q = AL^\alpha T^\beta K^\gamma$$

where A is a shift parameter, Q is output, and the exponents of the various factors are the respective efficiency parameters such that

$$h = \alpha + \beta + \gamma \lessgtr 1$$

Our purpose is to explore the relationship between the homogeneity parameter, h, and internal/external returns to scale. It is well known that returns to scale internal to the plant are reflected in the efficiency parameters of the production function. The purpose of an earlier section of this chapter was to identify a variety of factors which lead to external technological agglomeration economies. The most important of these factors are based upon specialization and indivisibilities. The point is that specialization and indivisibilities in production lead to conglomeration not only of the activity under consideration but also of activities which are vertically linked to it and to interindustry concentration as well. These various technological external economies are 'picked-up' by their locational effects on the efficiency parameters of the production function.

In any metropolitan area, some parcels of land are more favourably located than other parcels. Reasons for this include better accessibility to natural resources, labour and product markets, other production units, and some combination of these. There are several ways to represent this heterogeneity formally. One is to assume that several variables related to accessibility, which occasion a reduction in transport inputs utilized, enter the production function as separate arguments. A more fruitful way, given data availability, is to assume that different sites have associated with them different efficiency parameters in production functions.

The existence of internal scale economies together with the locational effects on efficiency parameters resulting from external scale economies function in such a fashion as to justify the existence of metropolitan areas. There are, however, finite limits associated with the efficient size of the city. As population size increases the fringe of the urban area is pushed further out thereby requiring more transport inputs per unit of output. That is, a doubling of the metropolitan population requires more than a doubling of transport inputs utilized per unit of output since at least some inputs going into as well as some output from the point of production make longer trips. This diseconomy in use of transport inputs will operate to offset somewhat the increasing returns in production.

To sum, h, the homogeneity or total scale parameter consists of several distinct agglomeration forces: (1) internal scale economies; (2) localization economies; (3) urbanization economies; and (4) urbanization diseconomies. Under this specification of scale economies, production function analysis employing time-series data for a given industrial establishment in a particular SMSA is appropriate. These resulting estimates of total scale economies should not be taken as an end in-and-of-themselves. These estimated agglomeration parameters will be more meaningful if they can be decomposed into the relevant contribution contributed by internal scale economies as well as external economies and/or diseconomies. That is, we would like to know for any given industry, whether it is internal scale economies, localization economies, urbanization economies, or some combination of these various forces which account for total scale economies for establishment in that industry. Likewise, we would like to have some idea about the role played by internal large scale and/or urbanization diseconomies as well. For this purpose cross-sectional analysis (for a given industry across SMSA's) will be utilized.

3.4.3. Specifying the functional form

Several specific functional forms have been widely used both in theoretical and empirical research. They are the Cobb-Douglas, the fixed technical coefficients, and the constant elasticity of substitution (CES) forms. The CES function is more general in that it includes both the Cobb-Douglas and fixed technical coefficients production functions as special cases. In the development of the CES production function Arrow, Chenery Minhas and Solow (1961), consider the following problem: if it is given that a certain relationship exists between wages and output per man-hour, then what sort of production function rationalizes this relationship? Specifically, if it is given that

$$W = A\left(\frac{Q}{L}\right)^\beta \tag{3.1}$$

and, if it is postulated that

$$Q = F(K, L) \tag{3.2}$$

what is the specification of the functional form F? The authors made the following assumptions:

1. The unit characterized by Equation 3.2 behaves as if it were a perfect competitor in both the product and factor markets.
2. The function in Equation 3.2 is homogeneous of degree one.

The functional form generated by Equation 3.1 and assumptions (1) and (2) is given by

$$Q = F(K, L) = A[\delta K^{-\rho} + (1 - \delta)L^{-\rho}]^{-1/\rho} \tag{3.3}$$

where A is an efficiency parameter which changes output proportionately for given quantities of input; $(0 \leq \delta \leq 1)$ is a distribution parameter which determines the division of factor income; ρ is a substitution parameter and is related to σ, the elasticity of substitution parameter, as follows:

$$\sigma = \frac{1}{1 + \rho}, \ -1 \leq \rho \leq \infty \text{ since } 0 \leq \sigma \leq \infty$$

Dhrymes (1965) suggests a generalization of Equation 3.1:

$$W = AQ^\beta L^\gamma \tag{3.4}$$

which reduces to Equation 3.1 when $\gamma = -\beta$. Furthermore, Dhrymes assumes that the unit behaves as if it were a profit maximizer, but that the markets in which it operates are not perfect; and that the production function characterizing the unit is homogeneous of degree h. Thus:

$$Q = F(K, L) = L^h F\left(\frac{K}{L}, 1\right) = L^h F\left(\frac{K}{L}\right) \quad (3.5)$$

The first order condition for profit maximization is given by

$$\frac{\partial Q}{\partial L} = W\left(\frac{1 + \epsilon_1}{1 + \eta}\right) \quad (3.6a)$$

$$\frac{\partial Q}{\partial K} = r\left(\frac{1 + \epsilon_2}{1 + \eta}\right) \quad (3.6b)$$

where η, ϵ_1, and ϵ_2 are, respectively, inverses of the elasticity of demand for output, supply of labor, and supply of capital. The product exhaustion requirement requires that

$$rK + WL = Q \quad (3.7)$$

This implies, using 3.6a and 3.6b, that

$$\left(\frac{1 + \eta}{1 + \epsilon_1}\right)\frac{\partial Q}{\partial L}L + \left(\frac{1 + \eta}{1 + \epsilon_2}\right)\frac{\partial Q}{\partial K}K = Q \quad (3.7a)$$

But, homogeneity of degree h implies

$$\frac{\partial Q}{\partial K}K + \frac{\partial Q}{\partial L}L = hQ \quad (3.7b)$$

From 3.7a and 3.7b we must have

$$\frac{\partial Q}{\partial L}\frac{L}{Q} = \frac{1 + \eta}{1 + \epsilon_1} \cdot \frac{\epsilon_1 - \epsilon_2}{\eta + h\eta - 1 - \epsilon_1} \quad (3.7c)$$

But 3.7c implies that the elasticity of output with respect to labor is completely determined if we specify, for example, constant elasticity of demand for output and supply of capital and labor. To avoid this rigidity, Dhrymes specifies that not both equations 3.6a and 3.6b hold. In particular, he assumes that only 3.6a holds. According to Dhrymes 'this has the interpretation that capital behaves independently and therefore, that the economic unit "optimizes" only with respect to labor. In addition, the distribution theory envisaged in this model is a residual one; the wage bill is essentially determined by (Equation 3.6a) and capital gets what is left over.' The implication of this assumption is crucial to the measurement of scale economies. Ideally, we wish to observe points on the long-run average cost function of the plant, rather than deviations from this long-run curve, i.e., points on various short-run cost curves, which when taken together form the long-run curve. Indeed, the very definition of scale economies refers to movements along the long-run average cost curve and not to movements along various short-run curves. The assumption that the economic unit 'optimizes' with respect to labor only ensures that the first order conditions for profit maximization are identical in both the short- and long-run. The formal proof of this proposition is taken up in Appendix A.

From the foregoing assumptions. Dhrymes goes on to specify the following functional form of F:

$$Q = F(K, L) = C(t)[\alpha_1(t)K^{h\delta} + \alpha_2(t)L^{h\delta}]^{1/\delta} \qquad (3.8)$$

Thus, Equation 3.8 is a variant of the CES production function, homogeneous of degree h, which generates Equation 3.4:

$$W = AQ^\beta L^\gamma \qquad (3.9)$$

Equation 3.9 can be rewritten as

$$W = A\left(\frac{Q}{L^h}\right)^\beta L^{\gamma+\beta h} \qquad (3.9a)$$

and as a matter of notation put

$$s(h) = \gamma + h\beta \qquad (3.9b)$$

It is desirable that Dhrymes' model reduces to that of Arrow, et al., whenever $h = 1$ and the perfect competition assumption holds. This requires that

$$s(1) = 0 \tag{3.9c}$$

The only linear functional form given to s which guarantees 3.9c and leads to a CES-like production function homogeneous of degree h in capital and labor is

$$s(h) = h - 1 \tag{3.9d}$$

Setting 3.9b and 3.9d equal, yields

$$h - 1 = \gamma + h\beta$$

Solving for h

$$h = \frac{1 + \gamma}{1 - \beta}$$

Appendix A demonstrates first that the production function given by Equation 3.8 generates Equation 3.9. In addition, Appendix A shows that by assuming that only the first marginal condition holds, Equation 3.6a, ensures that the short-run and long-run optimization problem is identical.

As noted by Dhrymes (1965:361-362) the CES-like production function has all the usual properties and is capable of dealing with or accounting for disembodied technical change. However, the derivation of the production function makes it difficult to distinguish (nonneutral or neutral) technical change from market imperfections. For our purposes sorting technical progress from market imperfection is not important. What is important is segregation of economies of scale and technical change. Appendix A also demonstrates that by assuming disembodied technical progress the homogeneity parameter, h, is a 'pure' scale measure. One problem that could arise in empirical application of the Dhrymes technique is that the estimate of the homogeneity parameter could be quite inexact for those industries in which embodied technical progress abounds.

3.4.4. The empirical model

The foregoing section suggests that, h, the returns to scale coefficient, can be estimated by applying ordinary least squares to the logarithmic transformation of Equation 3.9.[4] Moreover, data on capital (which is known to be quite scarce and often inadequate, if at all obtainable) are not required. In addition, for regional analysis the assumption of perfect competition is inappropriate since space itself and the existence of transport costs limits competition. Therefore, market structures characterized by imperfect competition are more appropriate. Furthermore, production function analysis is the appropriate technique given our theoretical construct. These are the primary reasons why we have elected to use Dhrymes' model in the empirical investigation.[5]

More precisely, in conducting the empirical analysis, data on wages, output, and labor for the i-th two-digit SIC industry in the j-th SMSA are fitted to the logarithmic transformation of Equation 3.9, yielding estimates of the agglomeration variable h_{ij}. In this study we employ 68 SMSA's (these various SMSA's are listed in Appendix B) and 19 industries (SIC 20-39, except SIC 21). Therefore, a series of estimated scale coefficients for each of the 19 industries is obtained, where data are available, for the 68 SMSA's considered in this work. For example, considering SIC 20, food and kindred products, an estimate of the agglomeration economies for the Boston SMSA is obtained. Likewise the estimated scale coefficient is also obtained for the Pittsburgh, New York, Chicago, San Diego SMSA's, etc. This, then, provides us with a series of estimated scale coefficients, $\hat{h}$, for SIC 20 for the various SMSA's under consideration. Similarly, a series of estimated scale coefficients for SIC $-22, \ldots,$ SIC -39 across the various 68 SMSA's is obtained.

Next, we decompose these measures of total scale into components which will explain how industries are affected by the various economies and/or diseconomies, if at all. To do this our estimated scale coefficients are employed as dependent variables in an industry-by-industry cross-sectional regression model designed to decompose the total scale economy measure into; (1) internal economies of scale (LSE_{ij}); (2) localization economies (LOC_{ij}); (3) urbanization economies (UBE_{ij}); and urbanization diseconomies (UBD_{ij}). This is,

$$h_{ij} = f(LSE_{ij}, LOC_{ij}, UBE_{ij}, UBD_{ij}) \qquad (3.10)$$

The primary drawback to disaggregating agglomeration forces is empirical rather than theoretical. Data for the various agglomeration economies and diseconomies are non-existent, therefore, a set of proxies must be developed which attempts to capture these various forces. The theoretical section of this chapter suggests the following sorts of proxies:

1. *Internal scale economies* (LSE_{ij}) – Labour employment of the i-th establishment located in the j-th SMSA could be utilized as a proxy for internal scale economies in the cross-sectional model. The total number of workers in the establishment is a proxy for internal scale economies most commonly used in econometric production studies, and it is also the one chosen here. Capital stock, total raw material usage or even gross or net production might serve equally well as a measure of size. Total labor employment is chosen because it is considered to be a more reliable measure (containing fewer errors of measurement than capital and it is measured in physical units as theoretically required rather than in monetary units as is output). A positive and significant sign attached to the coefficient of this variable would indicate that internal scale economies are important, whereas a negative and significant size implies internal diseconomies of scale apply.
2. *Localization economies* (LOC_{ij}) – As the relative concentration of an industry increases in a particular area, the possibility that economies which are external to the plant but internal to its industry may develop. One approach to measuring the concentration of an industry in a particular area relative to its national presence is the location quotient technique. Thus for industry i located in the j-th SMSA:

$$LOC_{ij} = \frac{X_i^j / \sum_i X_i^j}{X_i^n / \sum_i X_i^n}$$

where X_i^j represents the regional (SMSA) output or employment of industry i, $\sum_i X_i^j$ the total regional output or employment, X_i^n

the national output or employment of industry i, and $\Sigma_i X_i^n$ the total national output or employment.

Whether we choose employment or output to calculate the location quotient makes little difference. As the scale of the industry in a given area increases relative to the nation, our *a priori* reasoning leads us to expect a positive and significant sign attached to the coefficient for the localization economies variable.

Actually, several variables were experimented with during the empirical investigation. As well as location quotients for output and employment, the absolute level of industry output, employment and number of establishments in the industry located in the *j*-th SMSA were tried. Generally, the location quotient approach using SMSA manufacturing industry employment relative to national manufacturing employment in that industry gave best results, and was therefore chosen.

3. *Urbanization economies* – As the number of establishments in all industries taken together in the *j*-th SMSA increases, the possibility for economies of scale internal to the urban area becomes likely. Here location quotient techniques do not apply. Rather, one might choose to construct a distance decay agglomeration variable. The idea here is that SMSA's which are in a close geographical proximity might benefit from the external economies generated in these nearby cities.

A general index of urbanization economies for the *i*-th SMSA is defined by the following potential type variable, in terms of total number of all establishments and distance, d, among SMSA's

$$UBE_i = \sum_j \sum_t E_j^t / d_{ij}$$

where i and j now stand for the various SMSA's comprising this study and t the various establishments found in these SMSA's. Note that $d_{ij} = 1$ whenever $i = j$. Thus, UBE_i is larger: (1) the greater the number of all establishments in i; (2) the greater the number of all establishments in j; and (3) the shorter the distance between i and j.

While the agglomeration potential variable just described seems reasonable enough, it is not easily implemented. To construct this variable for our purposes, almost 6,000 individual pieces of data are required to build the mileage matrix, $[d_{ij}]$, alone. An alternative, which is less hungry in its data requirements, is to limit the geographical spread of these potential agglomeration economies. Bopp and Gordon (1977) suggest that 100 miles defines a 'generous limit for the radius for a major urban industrial complex.' While we are not dealing with industrial complex analysis the point is much the same – a 100 mile radius or any radius for that matter, appears arbitrary without additional empirical evidence to support it. Moreover, in what units should the d_{ij}'s be measured? We could simply use road mileage, but this assumes that there are no long-distance economies involved, i.e., the distance function is linear. Instead we could choose to measure distance in terms of travel time or 'social distance,' however defined. But then we must assume that travel time or social distance is uniform for all of the various types of urban agglomeration forces relevant for manufacturing activity. For reasons of this sort, the decision was made to employ the total number of reporting units found in the j-th SMSA as a proxy for urbanization economies for the i-th industry located in j. A priori a positive and significant sign is expected for the coefficient attached to this variable, if urbanization economies apply.[6]

4. *Urbanization diseconomies* (UBD_{ij}) – Large concentrations incur diseconomies such as increased utilization of transportation resources both to bring inputs to and ship output from the point of production. Likewise, as population increases less productive land becomes available as an input into the production process, which shows up as a diseconomy of scale. This suggests that urban population size could be used as a surrogate, in our model, designed to capture the influence of urbanization diseconomies. Here a negative and significant sign is to be expected, if urbanization diseconomies are relevant.

An equation such as (3.10) together with the proxies developed above should provide some insight into the agglomeration phenomenon. Equation (3.10) is designed to tell us for each manufacturing industry which combination of these various agglomerative forces add to an explanation of total scale economies for that industry. It would be nice if we could compare the magnitudes of the estimated coefficients, thereby enabling a comparison of the relative contribution to total scale economies from each of the various agglomeration forces. This, unfortunately, will not be possible, Since, for example, urbanization economies are measured as total reporting units in the j-th SMSA, while urbanization diseconomies are measured in terms of urban population size. To attempt to compare these estimated coefficients would be much like comparing apples to oranges. We can, however, examine the signs on the statistically significant coefficients, to see if these signs are consistent with our *a priori* hypotheses. In addition, those variables which are statistically significant suggest that these variables are important to any understanding and explanation of total agglomeration economies, as herein defined, for the industry under question.

The data sources, related data and estimation problems, as well as the statistical analysis will be discussed in the following chapter.

3.5 CONCLUSION

To summarize, a theoretical framework was developed which viewed indivisibilities as the major force leading to economies of scale in production and concentration or agglomeration of manufacturing activity in comparatively few urbanized centers. A variant of the CES production function was presented and proposed as a technique for measuring these agglomeration economies. Thus, scale economies for the various two-digit manufacturing establishments across SMSA's are estimated using time-series analysis. In turn, these estimates of total scale are utilized as dependent variables in a cross-sectional industry-by-industry regression model designed to decompose these estimates into the relevant economies and/or diseconomies.

CONCLUSION

NOTES

1. Actually, the shape of the demand curve depends upon a number of conditions as demonstrated by Greenhut and Ohta (1975). They show that the free spatial (regional) demand curve is convex to the origin regardless of the shape of the individual demands which make it up. The shape of the spatial competitive market demand curve depends upon the behavioral assumptions used in the competitive model. The linear demand curve drawn in fig. 3.3 is constructed as such for convenience.
2. The scenario described above is overly simplified to highlight the main features of the Lösian system. Questions regarding the entry of new firms when pure profits exists such as: how many, where will they locate, what impact will these new firms have on the location, size and shape of existing firms, and ultimately what will the equilibrium configuration of firms in space look like, have been ignored. For a more complete discussion of these and related questions see Segal (1977).
3. Robinson (1953–4:47) For an excellent discussion of the Cambridge Capital Controversy see Harcourt (1972), and Harcourt and Laing (1971).
4. Actually, Equation 3.8 above which generates Equation 3.9 is based upon the assumptions in 3.5 and 3.6 provided that 3.9d holds as well.
5. Dhrymes' model has been employed by Shefer (1969; 1973) to investigate localization economies in two-digit manufacturing industries in the U.S. See the previous chapter for extensive criticisms of the Shefer analysis.
6. In much the same fashion a potential type variable for localization economies for the i-th industry in j can be defined. This variable would account for the intra industry agglomeration economies do to the presence of the *same* industry in nearby SMSA's. An example here is the potential localization economies for establishments in primary metals in the Pittsburgh and Youngstown SMSA's due to the large concentration of this industry in these areas. This variable, however, is subject to the same problems as the urbanization economies potential proxy described above.

4. The empirical investigation

4.1. INTRODUCTION

In the preceding chapter, we have developed and described the model intended for use in the empirical analysis. In this chapter we will discuss the data employed to estimate the model, related data and estimation problems, and finally the empirical results.

4.2. ESTIMATING SCALE ECONOMIES: THE TIME-SERIES MODEL

The analysis and results to be presented are based on time-series data covering the period 1957–1972, or some sub-period therein, depending upon data availability. The unit of observation is value added (output), payroll, and number of all employees for a given two-digit SIC enterprise in a given SMSA. The application is to an establishment level production function. Thus, we require the assumption that the production functions are identical for all firms comprising the industry for a given SMSA. Suffice it to say that we have by no means overcome the aggregation problem. In our investigations, we assume implicitly that each establishment produces a homogeneous product and uses homogeneous factor inputs— such as labor and capital. These assumptions have hardly been met by the two-digit SIC industries which represent more often than not, a wide range of products, each with its own unique type of input requirement. While this suggests a finer degree of disaggregation, data at the three- or four-digit breakdown are not available.

Data to fit the Dhrymes function were taken from both the Census of Manufactures and the Annual Census of Manufactures.[1] The data given in the Census pertain to the industry as a whole. Value added in the Census usage includes depreciation and is thus a reasonable approximation to the output data required in this type of estimation. The number of all employees series refers to the average number of employees reported and hence may be an overstatement of the true labor employment series in the case where part-time employment practices prevail. From these series the average wage was computed simply by dividing the real wage bill (payroll deflated by the industry's wholesale price index) by the number of all employees series.[2]

Initially, the scale parameters were estimated at the two-digit, SIC industry level in a given SMSA. While many of the estimated scale coefficients appeared to have acceptable values, many did not. For example, Boston and Baltimore are both port cities and one would not expect to find decreasing returns to food and kindred products in these cities. Yet $\hat{h}$ for Boston is .4381 and .9472 for Baltimore. Even more anomalous is the strong decreasing returns to food and kindred products obtained for Milwaukee and Minneapolis, .3238 for the former and .2688 for the latter.

One possible explanation for these unexpected results is that we have not controlled for the entry and/or exit of plants in a given industry in a given SMSA over time. For example, assume that there are N firms each of which are exactly alike, producing output in some industry and experiencing increasing returns to scale. Next, assume that output is increased over time not by expanding capital and labor in each of the N firms but rather by entry of M new firms which are exactly like the N existing firms. Now, even though the $N + M$ firms all experience increasing returns to scale, our estimation technique will erroneously indicate constant returns to scale for the industry as a whole.

To control for the entry and/or exit of plants data for the number of establishments by two-digit SIC groupings for each SMSA employed in this study were collected.[3] These data enable us to conduct our analysis at the *establishment* level rather than at the *industry* level as before. Thus:

wage rate W_{ij}
$$= \frac{\text{Total real payroll of the } i\text{-th industry in the } j\text{-th SMSA}}{\text{All employees of the } i\text{-th industry in the } j\text{-th SMSA}}$$

output Q_{ij}
$$= \frac{\text{Total value added in real terms for the } i\text{-th industry in the } j\text{-th SMSA}}{\text{Number of establishments of type } i \text{ in the } j\text{-th SMSA}}$$

labor L_{ij}
$$= \frac{\text{All employees of the } i\text{-th industry in the } j\text{-th SMSA}}{\text{Number of establishments of type } i \text{ in the } j\text{-th SMSA}}$$

As mentioned earlier we have by no means overcome the aggregation problem. Ideally, we would like to have data at the establishment level since we wish to have:

$$\begin{aligned} W_1 &= AQ_1^\beta L_1^\gamma \\ W_2 &= AQ_2^\beta L_2^\gamma \\ &\cdots \\ W_n &= AQ_n^\beta L_n^\gamma \end{aligned} \quad (4.1)$$

Applying the logarithmic transformation to (4.1):

$$\begin{aligned} \ln W_1 &= \ln A + \beta \ln Q_1 + \gamma \ln L_1 \\ \ln W_2 &= \ln A + \beta \ln Q_2 + \gamma \ln L_2 \\ &\cdots \\ \ln W_n &= \ln A + \beta \ln Q_n + \gamma \ln L_n \end{aligned} \quad (4.1a)$$

Aggregating:

$$\Sigma \ln W_i = N \ln A + \beta \Sigma \ln Q_i + \gamma \Sigma \ln L_i \quad (4.2)$$

or

$$\frac{\Sigma \ln W_i}{N} = \ln A + \beta \left(\frac{\Sigma \ln Q_i}{N}\right) + \gamma \left(\frac{\Sigma \ln L_i}{N}\right) \quad (4.2a)$$

However, the Census of Manufacturers does not publish the individual data as required but rather the following aggregate totals:

$$\Sigma W_i, \Sigma Q_i, \text{ and } \Sigma L_i$$

ESTIMATING SCALE ECONOMIES

Dividing these aggregate totals by the appropriate number of establishments and applying the logarithmic transformation yields:

$$\ln\left[\frac{\Sigma W_i}{N}\right] = \ln A + \beta \ln\left[\frac{\Sigma Q_i}{N}\right] + \gamma \ln\left[\frac{\Sigma L_i}{N}\right] \quad (4.3)$$

Thus, the desired equation (4.2a) is not the same as the estimating equation (4.3).

In general,

$$\ln\left[\frac{\Sigma X_i}{N}\right] \neq \frac{\Sigma \ln X_i}{N}$$

However, Maeshiro (1973:149a–149c) has shown that

$$\ln\left[\frac{\Sigma X_i}{N}\right] \approx \frac{\Sigma \ln X_i}{N} + \frac{\sigma^2}{2} \quad (4.4)$$

Where

$$\sigma^2 = \Sigma \left(\ln X_i - \frac{\Sigma \ln X_i}{N}\right)^2 \quad (4.4a)$$

Equation (4.4) can be rewritten as

$$\ln\left[\frac{\Sigma X_i}{N}\right] - \frac{\sigma^2}{2} \approx \frac{\Sigma \ln X_i}{N} \quad (4.4b)$$

Using equations (4.2a), (4.3), and (4.4b) we can write:

$$\ln\left[\frac{\Sigma W_i}{N}\right] - \frac{\sigma_W^2}{2} = \ln A + \beta\left(\ln\left[\frac{\Sigma Q_i}{N}\right] - \frac{\sigma_Q^2}{2}\right) + \gamma\left(\ln\left[\frac{\Sigma L_i}{N}\right] - \frac{\sigma_L^2}{2}\right)$$

rearranging

$$\ln\left[\frac{\Sigma W_i}{N}\right] = \ln A + \beta \ln\left[\frac{\Sigma Q_i}{N}\right] + \gamma \ln\left[\frac{\Sigma L_i}{N}\right] + (\sigma_W^2 - \beta \sigma_Q^2 - \gamma \sigma_L^2)/2$$

Letting $\alpha = (\sigma_W^2 - \beta\sigma_Q^2 - \gamma\sigma_L^2)/2$ we can write

$$\ln\left[\frac{\Sigma W_i}{N}\right] = \ln A + \beta\ln\left[\frac{\Sigma Q_i}{N}\right] + \gamma\ln\left[\frac{\Sigma L_i}{N}\right] + \alpha$$

letting t represent time we can now write

$$\ln\left[\frac{\Sigma W_i}{N}\right]_t = \ln A + \beta\ln\left[\frac{\Sigma Q_i}{N}\right]_t + \gamma\ln\left[\frac{\Sigma L_i}{N}\right]_t + \alpha_t \quad (4.5)$$

Thus, if we estimate an equation like (4.5) without the α_t term, and if α_t varies over time we get biased estimators for β and γ. If, however, α_t is constant over time and we estimate an equation like (4.5) without the α_t term the resulting estimators are unbiased.

A small test to determine whether or not α_t can be taken as constant over time was carried out. The Boston SMSA was chosen and the variance of wages, output, and labor were calculated for three independent time periods: 1958, 1963, and 1967.[4] From this we wish to test the equality of the variances for these three time periods. Therefore, the following hypotheses were tested separately for wages, output, and labor:

$$H_o: \sigma^2_{1958} = \sigma^2_{1963} = \sigma^2_{1967}$$

H_A: at least one is different

The Chi-square test was employed and it was found that in 35 out of 38 cases the null hypothesis was accepted. Thus in most cases estimating an equation like (4.5) while disregarding the α_t term results in unbiased estimators of β and γ. That is, applying the logarithmic transformation to

$$W_{ij} = AQ_{ij}^\beta L_{ij}^\gamma \quad (4.6)$$

yields

$$\log W_{ij} = \log A + \beta\log Q_{ij} + \gamma\log L_{ij} \quad (4.7)$$

ESTIMATING SCALE ECONOMIES

$\hat{\beta}$ and $\hat{\gamma}$ obtained by estimating (4.7) can be used in turn to estimate the homogeneity parameter as

$$\hat{h} = \frac{1 + \hat{\gamma}}{1 - \hat{\beta}} \tag{4.7}$$

Table 4.1 provides a SIC-code/manufacturing industry cross reference, while Table 4.2 gives the results of the time-series study. The numbers in parentheses are the associated t-statistics obtained using a formula found in Kendall and Stuart (1967:231–234). By employing a Taylor's expansion, Kendall and Stuart provide a formula for expressing the variance of a ratio such as

$$(1 + \hat{\gamma})/(1 - \hat{\beta})$$

TABLE 4.1. Industries at two-digit SIC level

SIC code	Industry
20	Food and kindred products
22	Textile mill products
23	Apparel and related products
24	Lumber and wood products
25	Furniture and fixtures
26	Paper and allied products
27	Printing and publishing
28	Chemicals and allied products
29	Petroleum and coal products
30	Rubber and plastic products (N.E.C.)
31	Leather and leather products
32	Stone, clay, and glass products
33	Primary metal industries
34	Fabricated metal products
35	Machinery, except electrical
36	Electrical machinery
37	Transportation equipment
38	Instruments and related products
39	Miscellaneous manufacturing

as:

$$\text{var}\left(\frac{1+\hat{\gamma}}{1-\hat{\beta}}\right) = \left[\frac{E(1+\hat{\gamma})}{E(1-\hat{\beta})}\right]^2 \left[\frac{\text{var}(1+\hat{\gamma})}{E^2(1+\hat{\gamma})} + \frac{\text{var}(1-\hat{\beta})}{E^2(1-\hat{\beta})} - \frac{2\,\text{cov}(1+\hat{\gamma},1-\hat{\beta})}{E(1+\hat{\gamma})E(1-\hat{\beta})}\right]$$

Taking the square root of this expression provides us with the standard error for $\hat{h}$, from which the t-statistic for $\hat{h}$ can be formed as:

$$t = \hat{h}/\sqrt{\text{var}\left(\frac{1+\hat{\gamma}}{1-\hat{\beta}}\right)}$$

Other statistics such as $\bar{R}^2$, the Durbin-Watson, etc. are not provided due to space constraints.[5] We can, however, offer the following comments. Gernally, a good fit was obtained. In our results, rarely does $\bar{R}^2$ fall below .9. Time-series data is, however, traditionally characterized by high values for $\bar{R}^2$. One problem which could arise when employing time-series data is serial correlation of the residuals. In this study, the Durbin-Watson statistic was used to indicate the possibility of serial correlation. If serial correlation was indicated, generalized least squares was utilized, otherwise the ordinary least squares results were reported.

Table 4.2 is a convenient way of reporting the time-series estimates for two reasons. First, going across any row of the table gives the estimated returns to scale coefficients for the various industries found in those cities for which data were available. Second, reading down any column shows how the returns to scale coefficients differ for a given industry across the various SMSA's making up this study.

From either a rows or columns point of view, one rather consistent observation can be made – namely that the estimated scale coefficients are at times greater than unity in value, but in many instances these estimated scale parameters are found to be less than one in value. This 'mixed-bag' of results is to be expected. Metropolitan places can be characterized as concentrations of various activities.

Concentrations of economic activity are not homogeneous in attribute or mix, even in cities of similar population size. Thus, metropolitan locations are agglomerations of quite different sorts, offering differing agglomeration economies and diseconomies to an average establishment in the same industry.

At this point one might ask, however, how it is possible for establishments experiencing decreasing returns in one city to be competitive with similar establishments enjoying increasing returns in another city. Moreover, why don't those establishments which experience decreasing returns to scale in one city simply relocate, in the long-run, to cities offering increasing returns? An answer to the first query might include the following reasons: a representative establishment experiencing decreasing returns to scale in the j-th SMSA could have a sheltered market area which permits it to be competitive with more efficient production units in other nearby SMSA's. In addition, while similar establishments operate at different levels of scale, their average cost of production could nonetheless be quite similar. To see this, consider fig. 4.1 where two production units A and B are depicted. For simplicity of exposition these two units are assumed to have identical LAC curves. Establishment A operates in the increasing returns to scale portion of the LAC curve; producing Q_A units of output at an average cost of C_1 per unit. Establishment B operates, however, in the decreasing returns to scale range of the LAC curve producing Q_B units of output, but experiencing identical per unit cost to Establishment A (the more efficient production unit).

Regarding the second question as to the relocation of units over time, one must keep in mind that we are not trying to explain the locations of manufacturing activity. To explain manufacturing location requires additional information on market orientation, material orientation, etc., for the various units under consideration. With this additional information total orientation and the relative importance of agglomeration in locational choice can be analyzed. Just this sort of approach is taken by Latham (1976). Our purpose is somewhat different. The relative importance of agglomeration economies for the location decision is taken axiomatically. The justification of this is the voluminous theoretical and empirical literature on the relative importance of agglomeration economies to an understanding of manufacturing location. Given this, our purpose is two-fold: (1) to develop a more direct

TABLE 4.2. Returns to scale in two-digit manufacturing industry 1957–1972.

SMSA/SIC industry	20	22	23	24	25	26	27	28	29
Arron	.9680 (3.9076)							1.3310 (2.7401)	
Albany	.9191 (2.9400)	1.2346 (12.7693)	1.1269 (2.0654)			1.1734 (2.4190)	1.6223 (3.6393)	1.5563 (2.7776)	
Allentown	1.2583 (2.5530)	1.1730 (4.1137)	1.4157 (1.8095)				1.4473 (3.5517)	1.5091 (7.4628)	
Anaheim	.9724 (12.4352)						1.1465 (1.9420)	1.0240 (6.0206)	
Atlanta	1.0089 (3.0277)	.8412 (1.9629)			.6835 (2.2075)	1.5533 (1.5667)		1.3918 (7.4162)	
Baltimore	1.0719 (3.0215)		1.4072 (2.6900)		.9896 (1.3885)	.7759 (3.7369)	1.2554 (2.1800)	1.5175 (2.4016)	
Birmingham	1.0230 (2.1171)						1.7001 (2.5206)		
Boston	1.0850 (2.3587)	1.6279 (4.3350)	1.3353 (5.1542)		1.1892 (1.2915)	.9847 (3.6794)	1.3525 (4.0300)		
Bridgeport			1.0339 (3.9270)					.9451 (7.5696)	
Buffalo	.8030 (2.0829)	.8479 (2.3898)	.9000 (1.9781)		.5526 (1.4708)	.8630 (2.6726)	.9320 (1.0712)		.6667 (8.5509)
Canton	1.2360 (4.5508)					1.2166 (2.0936)	1.4285 (4.4782)		
Chattanooga	1.1250 (2.2445)	1.3864 (4.1251)						1.3845 (1.7329)	
Chicago	.9624 (2.8539)		1.0302 (3.1526)			1.1515 (2.8228)	.6677 (1.9984)	.9717 (2.3318)	1.0857 (8.6521)
Cincinnati	.8677 (2.1097)		1.0267 4.7678)		1.0412 (2.7430)	1.2334 (3.9124)		.5829 (4.7212)	.5725 (2.4691)
Cleveland	1.0116 (4.8372)	.7248 (2.1432)		.7161 (3.2266)	.9740 (3.3727)	1.2754 (4.1080)	1.1178 (2.8886)	.8030 (5.3720)	.7416 (3.3338)
Columbus	1.1955 (5.0315)				1.1795 (3.1837)	.8874 (2.0622)	.8463 (5.3085)		
Dattas	1.1706 (2.9097)		1.2167 (2.1316)		1.1468 (2.8507)		1.0441 (1.7461)	1.2358 (1.5100)	
Davenport	1.3601								
Dayton	1.0156 (2.5755)					1.2434 (2.7858)	.7116 (1.2471)		
Denver	1.6684 (2.9097)						1.0414 (1.4017)	1.1939 (5.8603)	
Detroit	1.0041 (7.2619)					1.0747 (3.4551)	.7347 (4.0173)		
Fort Worth	1.1367 (3.6802)						.9795 (1.7746)		
Gary	1.0253 (0.9596)						.6697 (4.7075)	1.4067 (2.2400)	.7003 (5.2939)
Grand Rapids	1.0299 (3.1780)				1.1426 (1.8136)		.6458 (4.9751)		
Greens Bopo	1.1348 (6.5636)	.6610 (3.0960)	.6242 (4.4574)		.8139 (1.4779)				
Greenville			1.0154 (2.4584)	.8724 (1.8525)				1.0410 (5.2635)	
Hartford	1.1326 (7.5816)	1.1515 (8.7079)				1.2496 (2.4253)	.9023 (4.1131)		
Houston	1.0317 (3.5898)		.9355 (2.6915)			.6913 (1.9746)		1.1403 (3.1270)	.7647 (8.2969)
Indianapolis	1.0826 (5.6814)					.9707 (2.9340)	.7116 (1.2471)	2.1818 (2.5129)	
Jersey City	1.9873 (1.3831)	1.8882 (5.0586)	1.1943 (1.6957)		2.1301 (0.6660)		.6700 (2.5690)	1.2674 (3.9297)	
Kansas City	1.2040 (6.8595)			.6680 (1.2053)			.8484 (0.9701)	1.2471 (5.0435)	

ESTIMATING SCALE ECONOMIES

30	31	32	33	34	35	36	37	38	39
.5692 (1.7758)				1.4761 (2.0753)	1.1802 (7.5557)				
		4826 (2.8466)	.6644 (1.8235)						
				1.0074 (1.4348)	1.0531 (3.1337)	.6857 (3.0783)			
.9247 (1.9824)				.7062 (2.8804)	1.0313 (2.1589)	.9022 (3.0703)	1.4631 (2.7864)	1.0764 (5.0309)	.9558 (5.483)
		1.6748 (2.6163)	1.4115 (9.1964)	.7448 (1.9827)	1.0135 (2.5037)	1.3181 (2.2764)	1.1520 (1.6322)		1.5710 (2.2670)
		.8943 (2.0935)	1.2269 (2.4714)	.8710a (2.0588)	1.3079 (2.5823)	1.2167 (3.4046)			
			.5605 (2.5470)				.7464 (3.3716)		
1.2021 (2.3738)	.8168 (2.7362)			.7353 (5.0687)	.9280 (4.1311)	.7073 (2.2627)	.8183 (3.7047)	1.5275 (4.4212)	1.6217 (2.5149)
1.0889 (2.4382)		1.4506 (2.4701)	.8686 (2.5725)	.8129 (8.1750)	.8910 (5.3218)	1.2154 a (2.2300)	1.1530 (1.6062)	.8337 (2.7429)	
.9181 (5.5774)			1.2684 (1.7707)	1.2796 (2.1335)	.7297 (2.9070)	.8994 (2.1591)	.9194 (5.0062)		1.2492 (2.327)
.8747 (2.4531)		1.0793 (6.5548)	1.1464 (2.7242)	1.4549 (3.7628)	.7666 (3.8316)				
		.7869 (2.6889)	.8699 (5.1646)	.7878 (3.6806)	1.2537 (2.9692)				
	.5359 (1.1819)	.7590 (1.9338)	.6809 (4.8615)	.8502 (2.6577)	.7555 (4.0661)	1.0792 (4.2487)	1.1368 (2.2876)		1.0584 (3.6516)
1.0776 (2.4655)			2.1854 (2.7416)	.9730 (5.0550)	.7516 (4.6266)	.8317 (1.0080)	.8543 (1.3737)		1.2113 (3.3670)
.5803 (1.7582)		1.0651 (1.9202)	.6739 (3.5637)	1.0866 (3.1587)	.9412 (4.7500)	.9680 (1.1375)			.7468 (1.8422)
1.1702 (5.5296)	.5981 (4.5914)		.9623 (0.7585)	1.2555 (2.2410)	.6408 (5.9881)	1.1215 (3.0982)	.6386 (2.1600)	.9366 (2.1850)	
				1.3427 (2.4562)	.7160 (2.0416)	1.3479 (2.1125)	1.1133 (4.9566)		
		.6518 (1.5669)	1.1123 (3.3812)		.7089 (2.6601)				
.9651 (3.7087)			1.2092 (3.5858)	1.2246 (2.0154)	1.0884 (7.4244)		1.3137 (4.8416)		
					1.3580 (5.5578)	.8505 (1.5746)			
.7112 (5.3500)		1.4055 (4.2185)	.5804 (0.9504)	1.1870 (3.5759)	1.1467 (6.7882)	.7047 (2.2687)	.7271 (2.5100)		1.0806 (3.3200)
				.9543 (1.3511)	1.0038 (1.5068)		.8500 (9.0611)		
		.7526 (2.5099)	1.3943 (2.8612)	1.9319			1.0398 (5.9271)		
			1.1766 (2.7100)	(2.7887) .8444 (2.9827)	1.0632 (2.2300)	1.2584 (3.4841)	.8864 (5.4255)		1.5666 (1.9356)
					.9709 (5.1145)				
				1.3753 (2.3510)	1.4576 (1.3740)	1.7470 (2.2262)		.6130 (2.5787)	
		1.5684 (3.8506)	1.2438 (5.8153)	1.1757 (2.1698)	**.6820 (4.6376)**				
1.0272 (3.0011)		.5617 (0.9058)	.6861 (4.0738)	1.2610 (2.1206)	.8500 (4.6406)	.6099 (2.0002)	6.047 (2.0113)		1.0094 (2.1411)

TABLE 4.2. (cont.)

SMSA/SIC industry	20	22	23	24	25	26	27	28	29
Lancaster	.9890 (2.0413)	.7835 (1.1826)							
Los Angeles	1.3660 (2.7800)	1.1523 (2.8910)	1.4324 (3.3383)	.7501 (3.8750)		.7998 (1.9277)	1.3264 (4.2405)	1.0848 (4.0310)	.9255 (6.4706)
Louis Ville	2.0361 (3.8254)			.9875 (2.8674)	1.3180 (3.0853)	1.5189 (1.8377)	1.2073 (2.6747)	1.5741 (4.3889)	
Memphis	1.8798 (3.4973)			.5627 (3.3510)	1.0333 (2.1550)	1.5917 (2.4918)	1.4659 (2.4928)	.9780 (2.6603)	
Milwaukee	1.7998 (3.1133)	1.1838 (2.0906)	1.2053 (3.3450)	.7730 (2.9302)	1.3681 (2.1855)	.7177 (3.3614)	1.0253 (3.1780)	.9201 (2.1840)	
Minneapolis	.8660 (2.9791)		.6053 (1.3822)	.9863 (2.9285)	1.0171 (2.5450)		1.2810 (2.8701)	.8306 (1.4318)	.5317 (1.2761)
Nashville	.8615 (1.8347)		.7496 (2.8008)				.7153 (1.9140)	1.3663 (1.7778)	
Newark	1.9464 (1.8811)		1.8725 (2.9863)		1.5945 (3.3402)		1.2688 (3.0333)	1.4809 (3.7000)	
New Orleans	.8518 (3.3255)		1.6064 (1.5603)				1.4283 (3.8840)		1.2815 (4.8550)
New York		1.8043 (2.3109)	2.3618 (2.4830)	1.4467 (2.0131)	.9012 (2.7235)	1.9314 (5.6812)	.9680 (3.0336)	2.0360 (4.7044)	
Paterson	1.5922 2.5725	.8552 0.3423	.8599 1.8714			1.7620 1.9419	.8152 2.9964	2.2003 1.9086	
Peoria	1.6062 (2.2364)					.5681 (0.5766)			
Philadelphia	.9944 (2.4857)	.8666 (5.5817)	.9671 (1.6424)		.9333 (2.2177)	1.5271 (2.8461)	.7909 (1.8524)	2.0413 (5.9066)	.5512 (8.5917)
Phoenix	.6790 (3.6802)						1.4607 (2.3800)		
Pittsburgh	1.0333 (2.7405)		1.7621 (1.4913)				1.7001 (2.5086)	1.4494 (6.6852)	
Portland	.8080 (1.5149)		.7450 (2.1904)	1.0428 (1.4422)	1.3848 (3.4550)	.7587 (2.4261)		1.5873 (6.4040)	
Providence	1.3598 (3.5772)	.8373 (2.4336)					.7140 (1.0925)		
Reading	1.1616 (6.6223)	1.2466 (3.8974)	.8803 (3.3450)			.9597 (1.2380)		1.2453 (1.5878)	
Richmond	1.1130 (2.9165)		.9038 (1.6770)			1.2744 (2.1671)	1.2549 (2.0260)	1.3861 (2.4470)	
Rochester			1.2107 4.0432)			1.3726 (3.3703)	.7366 (2.2968)		
Rockford	1.1249 (2.1272)								
St. Louis	1.3914 (5.8421)				.6907 (1.0350)		1.2810 (2.8701)	1.8714 (1.8044)	
San Diego							.8988 (2.1356)		
San Francisco	1.0188 (1.9754)		1.1071 (3.3976)	.6923 (4.1140)		1.0428 (2.0835)	1.0198 (8.9052)		
San Jose	1.3361 (0.7075)						.8807 (2.7078)		
Seattle	.7566 (1.0021)		1.0830 (1.9877)	.9020 (4.1876)		.6061 (1.9192)	1.1666 (1.4908)	.5055 (2.1575)	
Springfield	.7656 (1.9470)	1.0389 (4.5032)	.6604 (2.3442)			.9837 (1.5867)		.7949 (3.0631)	
Syracuse	1.2654 (4.9082)					1.1960 (5.3185)	.5801 (3.1407)	1.3718 (1.5029)	
Toledo	.8781 (10.9439)					1.4639 (6.6157)	.9652 (3.3843)	.8543 (5.1891)	.7318 (8.9649)
Utica – Rome	1.2019 (3.3926)	1.0573 (2.9781)			1.5875 (4.5386)				
Wichita	1.2087 (4.7501)								

ESTIMATING SCALE ECONOMIES

30	31	32	33	34	35	36	37	38	39
	1.5207 (2.4873)		.9523 (3.1007)	.9944 (62.7043)	.8113 (2.1462)	.5957 (0.2355)			.6052 (2.8285)
		1.2252 (1.9070)	.7088 (1.7984)	1.1313 (4.2805)					
	.5254 (2.1715)	.9735 (0.1453)		.5064 (0.6108)	.6318 (1.8703)	.6204 (13.2842)			
.6983 (1.1044)		1.1295 (2.6206)	.5957 (1.1310)	.6671 (1.9531)	.7357 (1.9700)	1.1432 (1.2966)	1.3313 (2.6439)	1.6814 (2.2414)	1.3615 (3.6861)
		.9770 (2.6781)			.8236 (1.9052)				
	1.5040 (2.9434)		1.3086 (3.7759)	1.3958 (7.0039)	.6659 (3.5773)	.8000 (3.3557)		1.1108 (2.1642)	
			1.5231 (0.9407)	.9200 (1.0290)	.9165 (3.0412)	1.1201 (2.3021)	1.1250 (2.2283)	1.0081 (3.7924)	1.1622 (6.2592)
		1.2313 (2.2307)					1.0600 (4.0371)		
1.1414 (2.5896)	1.1226 (2.3395)	1.5100 (2.5193)	.8235 (2.0002)	1.8172 (1.9223)	.6932 (2.6288)	.5499 (1.0650)	.6940 (6.8876)	1.1804 (2.2837)	
		1.8945 (3.0983)					1.1075 (1.2054)		
.7367 (0.8115)	1.9254 (3.0734)	1.5319 (2.1127)	1.7104 (1.8155)		1.9126 (2.8179)	2.0888 (1.1984)	1.5656 (2.6043)	1.3799 (2.2400)	1.8931 (3.5984)
.6049 (29.577)		1.2954 (2.5605)	.7842 (1.4641)	1.0700 (1.6137)	1.3758 (2.3193)	2.0531 (1.5814)		.9254 (1.1900)	1.0531 (3.8770)
.9395 (1.9999)	.6144 (2.8951)	1.4413 (1.7241)	1.0407 (1.7641)		.6000 (3.2454)	.9411 (0.9387)	.9357 (2.3750)	.6519 (2.0223)	1.0195 (8.0170)
				1.1861 (3.3616)	1.4478 (8.9182)	.8078 (2.5054)	1.3400 (3.3305)		
1.0826 (2.0438)		.7476 (2.0021)	.6257 (3.3603)	.6930 (2.0980)	.5700 (2.8467)	.8879 (1.9094)	.9475 (2.2062)	.7752 (4.4720)	.6649 (2.9801)
		.8296 (3.4334)		.7000 (3.0264)	1.6523 (4.1492)	1.1764 (2.8297)	1.1168 (3.7446)		
.7409 (4.9722)			.9466 (2.9908)	1.4254 (2.7570)	1.0787 (3.7572)	.7044 (0.2048)		1.4090 (1.5593)	
	1.2650 (2.8740)		1.5366 (4.0471)	1.0548 (5.3090)	.7481 (2.5722)	1.4931 (2.1232)	.9816 (1.2235)		
				1.5191 (2.5997)	.8832 (1.5147)	.7232 (2.2330)			1.1107 (3.1446)
				.8851 (2.1588)	.9907 (16.7576)		.7730 (3.6089)		
	1.0575 (3.0840)	1.0660 (2.7860)	1.2773 (3.1270)	2.0584 (4.2998)	.7419 (0.8095)	1.4061 (6.6362)	1.0415 (4.6785)	.7049 (2.0094)	1.1409 (2.8584)
					.9863 (5.1982)		.9736 (2.9316)		
.6152 (0.3357)		1.0249 (2.2231)	1.0451 (2.2666)	.9591 (2.0443)	.5728 (2.3116)	.9647 (2.4805)	.7649 (3.0560)		1.2940 (2.8980)
				.7367 (2.1954)		1.4627 (1.6245)			
		1.2000 (1.2222)		.8422 (1.0742)					
.8095 (1.5050)			1.0368 (5.4292)	.7524 (1.6286)	.6037 (2.3893)	.5459 (3.4040)			1.3625 (5.7851)
		.7416 (2.7715)	1.2462 (5.7668)	1.0094 (2.1930)	.8735 (16.2734)				1.0498 (2.3882)
		1.0228	.8955	.6077	.4804	1.2831	1.1186		

TABLE 4.2. (cont.)

SMSA/SIC industry	20	22	23	24	25	26	27	28	29
Wilkes-Barre	1.3391 (2.5454)		.9058 (2.2912)						
Worcester		1.0479 (3.2707)				1.6597 (1.3623)	1.0380 (3.1678)		
York	.9718 (3.3323)		.8030 (2.8141)		1.3193 (2.0004)	1.1010 (2.4958)	1.1448 (3.4506)		
Youngstown		1.1487 (3.4778)					.8893 (4.1629)		

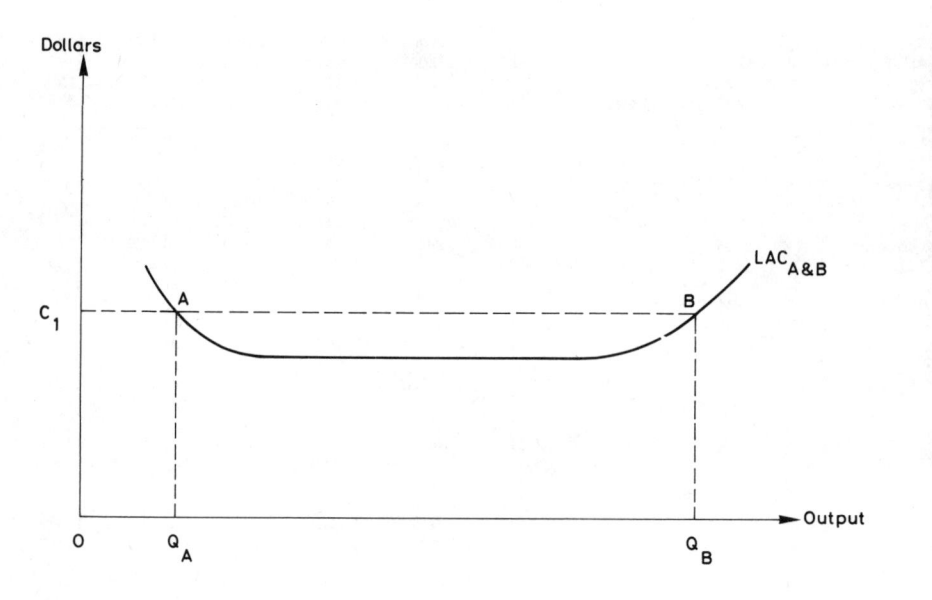

Fig. 4.1.

measure of the agglomeration economies variable then heretofore attempted; and (2) to employ (1) in such a fashion as to gain insight into which of the various agglomeration economies identified, if any, seem to be important for each of the manufacturing industries studied. The wide variation in the estimated scale

ESTIMATING SCALE ECONOMIES

30	31	32	33	34	35	36	37	38	39
		(1.0834)	(3.0703)	(4.8808)	(1.3574)	(3.3958)	(2.3767)		
			.5130	.7209					.6886
			(2.6872)	(1.8400)					(7.0439)
				.9483					
				(16.2260)					
	.8607								
	(2.6473)								
	1.2653		1.1105	1.4749	.7144				3.0103
	(4.7681)		(3.4676)	(3.3475)	(4.0663)				(6.0875)
	1.0244		1.4610	1.2512	.8794	1.2648			
	(4.4146)		(2.1167)	(2.7663)	(0.6512)	(4.3516)			
			.8273	6.3323	.5223	.9751	1.1078		
			(4.7285)	(2.2283)	(2.3799)	(1.9258)	(2.4506)		

parameters for a given industry across SMSA's supports the hypothesis that different areas offer a different 'mix' of the various agglomeration economies and diseconomies, which could exert a relative locational pull on manufacturing activity. It is the purpose of the cross-sectional empirical model to shed light on the importance of this mix by industry. This will be taken up shortly.

Returning to the question as to why units which are experiencing decreasing returns to scale in one area do not, in the long-run, relocate to areas offering increasing returns to the industry under consideration seems obvious. There is more to the location decision than the agglomeration economies offered by different metropolitan places. It is possible for units which are subject to diseconomies of scale in one area not to relocate to an area more favorable from an agglomeration economies point of view since these diseconomies could be more than offset by market, material, and/or other forms of orientation.

We now turn to an examination of the various rows of Table 4.2, i.e., how the estimated homogeneity parameters vary across industries in a given SMSA. It is interesting to note that the values of these estimated scale coefficients, for an average establishment in most industries, were among the largest in the New York SMSA. In addition, in only two out of the fifteen industries studies for the New York SMSA, were slight decreasing returns to scale indicated. Otherwise, the New York SMSA exhibited strong increasing returns to scale by industry. This result lends support to the view held by Vernon (1960) that strong external economies are present for manufacturing activity in New York. For the other extremely large SMSA's employed in this study (Chicago and Los Angeles) somewhat of a 'mixed-bag' of results was displayed. That is, for an average establishment found in either the Chicago or the Los Angeles SMSA's the estimated scale coefficients were at times greater than unity in value, but with almost equal incidence, the estimated scale parameters were found to be less than one in value. To reiterate, this 'mixed-bag' tends to be a general finding across industries for most of the SMSA's which comprise this study.

Table 4.2 might be useful in providing insight into Chinitz's (1961) hypothesis which related external economies to industrial structure. In Chinitz's view, external economies may be greater in cities such as New York which are highly diversified, than in cities such as Pittsburgh, Detroit, Gary and Youngstown, which are dominated by a single industry. The strong external economies indicated for New York are not the only source of evidence for the Chinitz hypothesis. Evidence for Chinitz's argument is also provided by the Pittsburgh SMSA in which the estimated scale coefficients for an average establishment were below unity for ten out of the thirteen industries studied. The 'mixed-bag' of results once again reappears for Detroit, Gary, and Youngstown. Clear-cut support for the Chinitz hypothesis was, therefore, not obtained.

In a somewhat different vein, the estimated scale coefficients of table 4.2 permit us to test empirically Equation 2.1 first introduced in Chapter 2

$$A_i = a + bP_i + cP_i^2$$

Using $\hat{h}$ as an estimate of A and SMSA population roughly averaged over the period of this study for P, we can test Equation 2.1 for the two-digit manufacturing industries employed in this study. The statistical unit is the estimated scale coefficient for a two-digit manufacturing unit, i, located in a single SMSA. The statistical universe (sample size) is a number of industries located in SMSA's, j, of various sizes. Thus

$$\hat{h}_{ij} = a + bP_j + cP_j^2$$

Support for the hypothesis that population provides a good proxy for agglomeration economies, while population squared serves as a measure of agglomeration diseconomies requires that

$b > 0$ and $c < 0$

If c differs from zero, an optimal city size exists found from

$P^* = b/2c$

Table 4.3 gives the results of the cross-sectional industry study. It gives the estimated coefficients and their associated t-statistics in parentheses. The results in Table 4.3 give no support to the hypothesis upon which the estimating equation is based. In 15 out of 19 cases the sign on $\hat{b}$ is negative; it is negative and significant in two instances. In no instance was the sign on $\hat{b}$ positive and significant as hypothesized. Likewise, an incorrect sign was obtained in 15 out of 19 industries for $\hat{c}$. Worse yet, in 7 cases the sign for $\hat{c}$ is positive and significant. Only once was the sign on c negative and significant as hypothesized.

The results of Table 4.2 support the point made in Chapter 2 that population scale of cities of various sizes in a poor proxy for business agglomeration economies and diseconomies of cities of different size. To summarize that argument, while population scale might serve as a reasonable proxy for household and social agglomeration economies, population scale is a worthless surrogate for business agglomeration economies. The latter tend to be related to industry size (localization economies) and/or inter-industry size (urbanization economies). Therefore, proxies which capture these influences are more appropriate.

4.3. DECOMPOSITION: THE CROSS-SECTIONAL MODEL

The preceeding estimation technique has provided us with an estimate of h_{ij}, the agglomeration variable, for a 'representative' firm in the i-th industry located in the j-th SMSA. The purpose of this section is to decompose these measures into components which will explain how industries are affected by the various economies and diseconomies, if at all. To do this, our estimates of the scale coefficients will be employed as dependent variables in a cross-sectional industry-by-industry regression model designed to decompose agglomeration externalities into: (1) internal scale economies (*LSE*); (2) localization economies (*LOC*); (3) urbanization economies (*UBE*); and (4) urbanization diseconomies (*UBD*).

TABLE 4.3. Increasing returns to scale and city size, 1957-72

SIC Code	Industry	Constant	Pop^1 ($\hat{b}$)	Pop^2 ($\hat{c}$)	R^2	Number of observation
20	Food and kindred products	1.20518	−.00004406 (−.433883)	.00004783 (.297180)	.0059	57
22	Textile mill products	1.16613	−.00009493 (−1.07162)	.00001372 (1.62120)*	.2387	20
23	Apparel and related products	1.03991	.00001481 (.180312)	.00000806 (1.03838)	.3053	33
24	Lumber and wood products	.99982	−.00013508 (−1.83998)*	.00001567 (2.48573)**	.6258	11
25	Furniture and fixtures	1.22740	−.00009037 (−.886099)	.00000554 (.62411)	.0847	20
26	Paper and allied products	1.29363	−.00015262 (−2.16177)**	.00001883 (2.70657)***	.2399	31
27	Printing and publishing	1.11084	−.00001124 (−.165533)	−.000000606 (−.87994)	.0131	44
28	Chemical and allied products	1.29375	−.000030774 (−.302106)	.0000076448 (.763588)	.0664	48
29	Petroleum and coal products	1.01122	−.0002486 (−1.31167)	.0000373 (1.45995)*	.2808	10
30	Rubber and plastic products	.834707	.00010072 (.587166)	−.00002076 (−.58287)	.0227	18
31	Leather and leather products	1.14026	−.00014212 (−1.14354)	.00001887 (1.71101)*	.3684	13
32	Stone, clay and glass products	1.14665	−.0000923 (−.111876)	.00000297 (.366875)	.0258	28
33	Primary metal industries	1.12038	−.00008868 (−1.02102)	.000011913 (1.41969)*	.0829	36
34	Fabricated metal industries	1.03326	.0001310 (1.11118)	−.00002668 (−1.47286)*	.0638	48
35	Machinery, except electrical	1.15241	−.00009422 (−.728138)	.00001221 (.624019)	.0183	35
36	Electrical machinery	1.15241	−.00009422 (0.728138)	.00001221 (.624019)	.0183	35
37	Transportation equipment	1.04340	−.00006670 (−1.30109)	.00001077 (2.12860)**	.2498	31
38	Instruments and related products	.89229	.00007438 (.692827)	−.0000023 (−.239294)	.1925	15
39	Miscellaneous	1.05475	−.0000204 (−.287587)	.00008275 (1.20857)	.2877	24

***indicates a .01 level of significance
**indicates a .05 level of significance
*indicates a .10 level of significance

More formally,

$$h_{ij} = f(LSE_{ij}, LOC_{ij}, UBE_{ij}, UBD_{ij})$$

where subscripts i represents the industry and j the SMSA under consideration. From the foregoing chapter we expect

$$\partial h/\partial LSE \lesseqgtr 0, \partial h/\partial LOC > 0,$$
$$\partial h/\partial UBE > 0, \quad \text{and} \quad \partial h/\partial UBD < 0$$

In the preceding chapter proxies for the various economies and diseconomies were developed. Typically, in cross-sectional analysis, data are analyzed for a single point in time. Here, rather than choosing a particular year, such as 1972, data were averaged over a business cycle of sufficient length. In particular, the data are averaged over the period 1961 to 1970 since this period corresponds to one complete phase of the cycle, i.e., reference dates from trough-to-trough are February 1961 to November 1970 [Business Conditions Digest (1972):114]. This should, in part, help overcome the capacity utilization problem, as the data are averaged over a business cycle.

Since the homogeneity parameter is relevant for a 'representative' establishment, the internal scale economies proxy used is average manufacturing employment in industry i, located in j, i.e., total manufacturing employment of industry i in j divided by total establishments of the i-th type in j. Data for employment are taken from the Census of Manufactures. Data for the number of establishments were obtained from two sources: the Census of Manufactures and County Business Patterns.

Data for the localization economy variable pertain to SMSA manufacturing employment in industry i relative to national manufacturing employment in industry i. Data on employment were obtained from the Census of Manufactures.

Turning to urbanization economies and diseconomies, the *total* number of reporting units in the j-th SMSA was used as a surrogate for the urbanization economies variable. These data were also found in County Business Patterns. Finally, as suggested by the Baumol-Mills hypothesis, population scale of the j-th SMSA was found to be, in general, the best proxy for capturing the influences of urbanization diseconomies.[6]

Initially the industry-by-industry cross-sectional model was estimated without consideration of possible 'frictions' between cross-sectional and time-series analysis. Generally, extremely poor fits (low values of R^2) were obtained. After some consideration it was realized that the time-series estimates of h introduced heteroscedasticity into the cross-sectional model. In the time-series study we assumed that the errors entered multiplicatively, that is,

$$W = AQ^\beta L^\gamma U$$

where U is the random disturbance term. Thus we can define

$$u = \ln U$$

We further assume that

$$u \sim N(0, \sigma^2)$$

That is, we assume that u is distributed normally with zero expectation and constant variance. The problem is that the homogeneity parameters, h's, are estimated from different samples, each of which is assumed to exhibit zero mean and constant variance for that sample, but the variances could differ from sample to sample. For example, consider $\hat{h}$ for two establishments in the same industry but located in different SMSA's. The homogeneity parameters which are estimated for each establishment have been estimated from different time-series samples. While each individual sample can be assumed to exhibit constant variance, it is unlikely that the variances will be constant among any of these samples. While this poses no problems for the estimation of the h_{ij}'s, it does, however, cause the familiar problem of heteroscedasticity of the error terms in the cross-sectional model. When heteroscedasticity is present, ordinary least-square estimation places more weight on the observations which have large error variances than those with small error variances. Due to this, the ordinary least-squares estimates are unbiased and consistent, but they are not efficient since the variances of the estimated parameters are not the minimum variances. In addition, the estimated variances of the estimated parameters will be biased estimators of the true variances of the estimated parameters. This has the disadvantage that standard test of significance will not apply.

If we have *a priori* knowledge about these variances, this knowledge can be used to employ weighted or generalized least-squares. When heteroscedasticity is present we can write

$$Eu_t^2 = \sigma^2 \lambda_i$$

where the λ_i's are the known constants. Thus, we can divide both sides of the regression equation resulting in the error term

$$u'_t = u_t/\sqrt{\lambda_i}$$

which satisfies the homescedasticity or constant variance requirement.

One problem still remaining is that we do not know the values of the λ_i's. We do, however, have sufficient information to estimate them. Since we believe that the λ_i's are proportional to the variance of h, we could employ the estimates of the variances of $h(\hat{\sigma}_h^2)$ to get an estimate of the λ_i's. The idea is that $\sqrt{\hat{\sigma}_h^2}$ is an unbiased estimate of $\sqrt{\sigma_h^2}$. To be sure the estimation procedure is not BLUE but it does take account of heteroscedasticity. This correction was, in addition, made to the data presented in table 4.3 above.

Table 4.4 presents the result of our cross-sectional analysis. The column on the extreme left of table 4.4 lists the industry under consideration. Columns headed (1)–(5) give the values of the estimated coefficients, while the numbers in parentheses are the associated *t*-statistics. Column (6) gives R^2, while column (7) lists the appropriate number of observations employed in the estimation process. Here, both the New York consolidated and the Chicago consolidated SMSA's were dropped from the analysis due to unavailability of data for some of the cross-section proxies. In addition, where the estimated scale parameters obtained in the time-series analyses failed to pass the test of statistical significance (a *t*-statistic significant at least at the .05 level), these estimated coefficients and their respective SMSA's were eliminated from the cross-sectional study.

We now turn to an industry-by-industry analysis of the results presented in table 4.4. One problem which should be mentioned at the outset is that the diversity of the product mix in all of the two-digit industrial groupings complicates the analysis. The wide range

TABLE 4.4. Decomposition of scale economies for the two-digit SIC manufacturing establishments

SIC code industry	(1) Intercept C	(2) LSE	(3) LOC	(4) UBE	(5) UBD	(6) R^2	(7) No. of Obs.
SIC 20 Food and kindred products	.796800 (9.97225)	10.2371 (3.81357)***	−.708217 (−.550343)	.0259237 (2.92001)***	−.00050929 (−3.15020)***	.9165	57
SIC 22 Textile mill products	1.24582 (11.1229)	−.550522 (−.498924)	−.236801 (−.240624)	.0202572 (2.35970)***	−.00041094 (−2.53024)***	.8974	20
SIC 23 Apparel and related products	.647277 (4.87808)	1.23475 (.929681)	.545769 (.915339)	.0131065 (1.52205)*	−.00015107 (−.876451)	.4510	33
SIC 24 Lumber and wood products	1.03703 (4.85928)	−2.09416 (−.456603)	−.350830 (−.140303)	.0210160 (1.97440)**	−.00046034 (−1.77833)*	.6213	11
SIC 25 Furniture and fixtures	1.23485 (4.71170)	2.53355 (.431336)	−3.80240 (−.905622)	.0141762 (1.46553)*	−.00036148 (−1.53487)*	.4682	20
SIC 26 Paper and allied products	1.16842 (4.87809)	−4.26892 (−1.19045)	8.17546 (1.53946)*	.0100884 (1.63886)*	−.00018925 (−1.35978)*	.6125	31
SIC 27 Printing and publishing	.907764 (6.40817)	−4.16400 (−.694345)	2.61190 (.994445)	.0035290 (1.71230)**	−.00007088 (−.677147)	.5809	44
SIC 28 Chemical and allied products	1.06689 (7.01145)	.067909 (.0196853)	−1.03367 (−.216100)	.0105754 (1.05061)	−.0001704 (−.788594)	.5714	38
SIC 29 Petroleum and coal products	.749381 (5.83285)	−.946206 (−.819391)	4.46335 (.752995)	.017828 (1.33034)*	−.00030194 (−1.19840)	.7818	10

SIC 30 Rubber and plastic products	.671826 (5.20981)	2.69288 (2.56451)**	−2.98326 (−3.06576)***	.0158002 (1.56428)*	−.00024054 (−1.68993)*	.8644	18
SIC 31 Leather and leather products	1.18217 (2.000887)	−3.15159 (−.725968)	1.13953 (.268614)	.0200125 (1.66929)*	−.0004170 (−1.55267)*	.2423	13
SIC 32 Stone, clay and glass products	1.99297 (6.35127)	−9.38767 (−2.14129)**	13.6860 (2.04010)**	.0016535 (.225139)	−.00000258 (−.174178)	.6052	28
SIC 33 Primary metal industries	1.05458 (.795141)	.795141 (1.85770)*	−2.00131 (−1.1817)**	.015684 (1.25859)	−.0003238 (−1.43222)*	.5887	36
SIC 34 Fabricated metal products	1.02365 (13.9872)	2.67893 (.885999)	−2.61366 (−1.71361)**	.0108574 (1.48467)*	−.0001965 (−1.44217)*	.9901	48
SIC 35 Machinery, except electrical	.906482 (7.44924)	−1.53205 (−2.92785)***	1.76851 (1.68384)***	.0099908 (1.03497)	−.0001580 (−1.11132)	.8799	35
SIC 36 Electrical machinery	.865953 (10.9411)	−2.5246 (−1.68124)*	1.32557 (2.02622)**	.00421524 (.636145)	.00009052 (−.748863)	.8830	49
SIC 37 Transportation equipment	.839054 (8.21910)	.182663 (.648410)	−.04933 (−.148536)	.00060407 (.844774)	.000004097 (.028109)	.3033	31
SIC 38 Instruments & related products	1.08825 (7.50758)	−7.76459 (−2.13407)**	17.8694 (2.16360)**	.0055685 (.805481)	−.00010573 (−.720818)	.6790	15
SIC 39 Miscellaneous	.983048 (7.52487)	5.18057 (.841222)	−10.9278 (−1.09255)	.0171128 (1.85356)**	−.00026373 (−1.55118)*	.7501	24

*** indicates a .01 level of significance
** indicates a .05 level of significance
* indicates a .10 level of significance

of products produced in any industrial classification suggests that many of the 'sub-industries' will have their own unique type of input requirements as well as sensitivity to the various agglomeration forces. This, in and of itself, should not invalidate the analysis but instead should only sound a warning in the acceptance and in the interpretation of the results.

4.3.1. SIC 20 Food and kindred products

This industrial group consists of establishments producing foods and beverages and certain related products (e.g., vegetable and animal fats and oils) for human consumption as well as prepared feeds for animals and fowls.

Table 4.4 indicates that internal scale economies are important in explaining total scale in this industry. Historically, the food industry has had more establishments than any other industry, but most of them were small in scale, whether measured by number of employees or value added. The small-scale nature of the industry can be explained primarily by the nature of the processes involved, the perishability of raw materials and finished products, as well as widespread markets. Recent developments, however, have brought about significant changes in the optimum size of food processing plants. According to the U.S. Department of Agriculture, the most important influence was a rapidly changing technology, which affected most of the operations of a food plant, e.g., materials handling; development of continuous processing as a substitute for batch operating; packaging; and automatic control of volume of flow.

At the same time, the baking industry tends to be small-scale and urban oriented. The baking industry produces a wide variety of products. Bread is the principal item of the division making almost exclusively soft-dough products, which include cake, rolls, pie, pastry, and doughnuts. Because bakers must deliver their bread almost immediately after it is produced, baking is a local industry. The geographical distribution of bakeries is almost identical with the distribution of the urban population. The most obvious explanation for the predominance of small shops is, of course, the nature of the product. The rapid perishability of bread restricts the size of the market which can be served. Since these firms are small and unable to internalize economies of scale they must rely upon the external economies large metropolitan areas offer. As our empirical results indicate, urbanization economies are an important source in explaining total scale in the food and kindred products industry.

Due to the fact that many of the items in this major grouping are highly perishable, they require specialized transportation equipment, e.g., refrigerated trucks and box cars. This implies that generally transportation resources used as inputs could be quite considerable. Inasmuch as transport resources used and population size are positively related, it is not surprising that the sign on the urbanization diseconomy proxy is negative and significant.

4.3.2. SIC 22 Textile mill products

The textile industries include all those mills which perform one or more of the processes involved in the manufacture of yarns and fabrics, such as spinning cotton, wool, silk, or rayon fibers into yarn; weaving or knitting yarn into cloth; finishing the fabric by dyeing, bleaching, or printing, etc.

Large-scale operations are less prevalent in the textile mill industries, as well as the absence of concentration (localization economies).[7] The absence of concentration and the presence of many small mills can be explained almost fully by the technique of production and the nature of the product. Unlike steel or aluminum production, for example, no process in textile spinning or weaving requires large-scale operations to be conducted economically. Increasing the size of mill does not result in any appreciable manufacturing economies.

All of this is quite consistent with our regression result, as neither internal scale economies nor localization economies were indicated. Urbanization economies as well as diseconomies, however, appear to operate. As indicated, large-scale operations are not prevalent for this industry and therefore the ability to internalize economies in the 'stock-piles' of, for example, inventories of specialized services is weak. This suggests that urban locations which can internalize these sorts of activities would prove to be attractive to these establishments.

4.3.3. SIC 23 Apparel and related products

This major group, known as 'needle trades' indicating that all the members of the group employ a common technology, includes establishments producing clothing and fabricated products by cutting and sewing purchased woven or knit textile fabrics and related materials such as leather, rubberized fabrics, plastic and furs.

Clothing manufacture is one of the least mechanized industries in the United States. The primary reason for this is that styles set limits beyond which machine processes cannot go. The fact that there are thousands upon thousands of designs developed every season involving numerous operations mitigates against the use of large specialized capital equipment. The average shop employs only about 40 workers.

It is in this vein that Hoover (1971:77–79) characterizes the apparel industry as small plants manufacturing garments, employing a long sequence of separate operations. One such operation is the cutting and binding of buttonholes. Specialized equipment exists for making buttonholes rapidly and cheaply in large quantities, but it represents a sizable investment. Any individual garment manufacture would not find it advantageous to invest in such a machine since he could not keep it busy all the time. If, however, he is located in a cluster with enough other garment manufacturers, their combined need for buttonholes may suffice to keep at least one of these specialized buttonhole machines busy. In that event, a separate firm specializing in buttonhole making could profitably join the cluster.

This example could be extended to cover other individual operations which likewise can be delegated to specialized firms when there is a cluster, e.g., zipper manufacturing.

Our empirical findings do not lend support to Hoover's intra-industry analysis, since we did not get a significant coefficient for the localization economies variable. Hoover is referring to the concentration of the garment industry in New York City. While the garment industry does seem to enjoy localization economies in New York, our empirical results suggest that localization economies cannot be taken as generally applicable to the apparel industry in all locations. Rather, our empirical analysis suggests than an important ingredient to total scale economies for this industry is urbanization economics (a positive and significant coefficient on the urbanization economies variable). Establishments in this industry tend to be small-scale operations. They, therefore, must rely upon the external economies, of the sort described in the last chapter, which large metropolitan areas offer.

4.3.4. SIC 24 Lumber and wood products

This group consists of logging camps engaged in cutting timber and pulpwood; merchant sawmills, lath mills, shingle mills, cooperate stock mills, planing mills, and plywood mills, and veneer mills engaged in producing lumber and wood basic materials; and establishments engaged in manufacturing finished articles made entirely or mainly of wood or wood substitutes.

According to the 1967 Census of Manufactures there are 16,334 logging camps and contractors in the United States. More than 13,000 of these are extremely small, engaging fewer than 5 employees each; some 3,000 employ between 5 and 99 persons, and only 41 employ more than 100. These numerous but small establishments are located near naturally growing forest timber and near timber which can be grown by agriculture.

Turning to secondary production which involves sawmills and planing mills, and veneer and plywood production, we see in these activities that there occur significant Weberian weight reductions on raw material inputs. Hence, processing installations are pulled toward the localized raw materials rather than urban centers.

Indeed, only 17.4% of total employment in SIC 24 was found in SMSA's in 1963.[8] This is the lowest ratio of SMSA to total employment in in any of the manufacturing industries.

The negative and significant sign on the urbanization diseconomy variable is consistent with expectation; large concentrations of populations repel establishments in this major grouping. In addition, the positive and significant sign on the urbanization economies variable suggests that establishments in this industry which are located in urban centers receive benefits from such a location, albeit they are few in number.

4.3.5. SIC 25 Furniture and fixtures

This grouping includes establishments engaged in manufacturing household, office, public building, and restaurant furniture; and office and store furniture.

Urban centers are playing an increasing role in the location of the furniture industry. Furniture is bulky, relatively heavy, and is easily damaged in transit. Transportation resource requirements are therefore heavy.

In the nineteenth and early twentieth centuries furniture centers were frequently oriented toward raw material sources. Today, many varieties of woods are used in the production of furniture, e.g., walnut, birch, maple, mahogany, cherry, etc. These must be assembled from a wide variety of areas. Consequently it requires less transportation input to bring raw materials to the point of production which is near the market than to produce furniture at a raw material source.

At the same time, the furniture industry is labor intensive. Thus, a large percentage of furniture manufacture is located in areas where a labor supply has developed over a long period of time.

This discussion suggests that urbanization economies could be relevant. The empirical results do indicate that urbanization economies offset by urbanization diseconomies are important to establishments under this heading. Urbanization diseconomies could be the result of the increased use of transportation resources necessitated in more populous urban centers. As indicated, transporting the final product to market is quite heavy in its transportation resource requirements.

4.3.6 SIC 26 Paper and allied products

This major group is composed of the manufacture of pulps from wood and other cellulose fibers, and rags; the manufacture of paper and paperboard; and the manufacture of paper and paerboard into converted products such as paper coated off the paper machine, paper bags, boxes and envelopes.

Pulp and paper production involves many different kinds of processes according to the nature of the product, ranging from kraft packing paper to specialized types of paper for fine books. Even though the industry is characterized by such diversity, our empirical findings suggest, however, that some general observations on the forces influencing total scale economies can be made.

Pulp mills tend to be small-scale operations, however measured. The percent of manufacturing employment is extremely low, and the value of its manufacturing shipments and value added are almost as low. Pulp mills tend to be raw material oriented for two reasons: transport costs on pulpwood are high relative to the transport cost of pulp; and there is no significant weight loss in the pulping processes. Pulp mills tend to be located heavily in the South and the Far West demonstrating some concentration characteristics. This could help to explain the positive and significant sign attached to the localization economies proxy.

When discussing pulp and paper, two other factors are of importance in the location of mills: an adequate water supply; and the pollution characteristics of this industry. The pulp and paper industry is the second largest industrial user of water. Therefore, pulp and papermill sites must be at points where there is adequate water supply. In terms of pollution, water pollution occurs as a result of heated and waste effluence, and noxious fumes are also emitted. These factors tend to keep mill sites away from major urban locations, and probably account for the negative and significant sign attached to the urbanization diseconomy variable.

Isolating on papermills, we find this activity to be extremely concentrated in the northeast of the United States, whether considered by actual number of establishments or by value added. Moreover, paperboard is the fastest growing and, from the standpoint of tonnage, the largest branch of the paper industry. Paperboard is made from a variety of raw materials, wastepaper and unbleached sulfate pulp being the most important from the standpoint of tonnage. Wastepaper may be used almost exclusively in the manufacture of low grades of paperboard (and more recently for production of recycled paper) where high finish and strength are unimportant. Therefore, companies which make great use of wastepaper have located their mills in or near large cities where ample quantities of wastepaper can be collected. This heavy concentration of the paper industry in the urban northeast most likely accounts for the positive and significant signs on both the localization and urbanization economies variables.

4.3.7. SIC 27 Printing and publishing

This collection of industries includes establishments engaged in printing by one or more of the common processes, such as letterpress, lithography, gravure, or screen; and those establishments which perform services for the printing trade, such as bookbinding, typesetting, engraving, photoengraving, and electrotyping. This grouping also includes establishments engaged in publishing newspapers, books, and periodicals.

Printing and publishing is labor-intensive relative to raw materials. Printing utilizes technical labor inputs which are obtainable only in the larger urban centers, and these also constitute the major markets for printing outputs such as books, magazines, and newspapers. Due to the immediacy of the consumption of newspapers, they must, at least for major sales volumes, be produced in, or adjacent to, major markets. In 1963, the ratio of SMSA to total U.S. employment stood at 72.1%, which is one of the largest ratios found among industrial manufacturing.[9] In addition, printing and publishing is surrounded by considerable uncertainty. In the publication of any periodical there is no way of telling in advance what resources will be needed to produce the copy and illustrations of any issue. This was succinctly put by Vernon (1960):

on short notice, a specialist on the politics of Dahomey and the Voltaic Republic, or the geography of Tibet, or on the properties of strontium 90 may have to be rounded up; library facilities which can disgorge the facts about the paleolithic era may be needed; and so may illustrators who can provide a credible version of the astronaut in flight.

This sort of uncertainty reinforces metropolitan locations where these highly specialized resources exist in abundance.

The empirical results given in table 4.4 do indicate that urbanization economies, as expected, are important in an explanation of total scale in this major grouping.

4.3.8. SIC 28 Chemical and allied products

The chemical industries produce an extremely large number of products, and the variety is increasing at a remarkable pace. Today, 40% of the chemical products produced in the United States were unknown in 1950. As a result it is difficult to classify the industry. The Census of Manufactures divides 'chemicals and allied products' into three major subgroups. These are (1) *basic chemicals*, such as acids, alkalies, and tonnage organic chemicals; (2) *chemical products* to be used in further manufacturing, such as synthetic fibers, plastics, solvents, and dyes; and (3) *finished chemical products*, such as drugs, paints, detergents, and fertilizers. The last two categories are sometimes classified as *fine chemicals*.

The estimation procedure was unsuccessful in turning up any significant coefficients. This could be due to the following observations. First, the chemical and allied industries consist of a vast number of establishments scattered all over the country. Most chemical plants are relatively small, i.e., employing less than 250 employees each. At the same time, a large percentage of employees work in large plants, which employ 2,500 or more workers. That is, the smallest and the largest plants together account for most of the workers in the industry. There is probably no such thing as an ideal plant size for the chemical and allied products because of the great variety of products or peculiar combination of products made in each plant.

More troublesome for our estimation technique is the fact that this industry is characterized by frequent changes in product and process and the concomitant rapid outmoding of plant and equipment (which implies embodied technical progress). Not only is technical progress embodied in the capital stock of this industry, but in labor as well. Even minor executives and salesmen must have received some formal training in chemistry. It is therefore relatively easy to build up a close liaison between the universities and the chemical companies and to equip the employees of the latter with the latest technical knowledge.

Since the Dhrymes technique cannot handle embodied technical change, which seems to be the rule in this industry, this could suggest why our empirical results are so poor.

4.3.9. SIC 29 Petroleum and coal products

Establishments under this heading are primarily engaged in petroleum refining, manufacturing paving and roofing materials, and compounding lubricating oils and greases from purchases materials.

The petroleum industry is dominated by large corporate enterprises engaged in all phases of the business from prospecting for crude oil to retail distribution of gasoline. In general it tends to be capital-intensive. More than one-half of its 437 establishments employ fewer than 100 workers and 80 find work for fewer than 5.

The large size of the establishment, as well as the high capital-labor ratio suggests that urbanization economies need not be important to this industry since the establishment can internalize many economies itself. Yet our statistical results indicate just the opposite, i.e., the coefficient on the internal scale economies variable is not significantly different from zero while the urbanization economies proxy variable is positive and significant. The actual distribution of refineries shows that in excess of 50% of refining capacity is along the Atlantic and the Pacific seaboards and the Gulf of Mexico. Seaboard refineries are in an excellent position to receive crude oil by pipeline from the nearby oil fields, and they are equally well located to receive foreign crude oil delivered by ocean-going tankers. Finished products such as gasoline and fuel oil are also transported economically by coastwise tankers from the Texas Gulf Coast refineries to the country's largest consuming area along the Middle Atlantic Coast in the New York and Philadelphia areas.

Indeed, metropolitan location for petroleum and coal products establishments is the exception rather than the rule. We were able to gather only 10 observations to employ for our cross-sectional analysis. The small number of observations could account for the unanticipated empirical results.

4.3.10. SIC 30 Rubber and plastic products (N.E.C.)
In this category we find establishments engaged in producing rubber products such as tires and rubber footware, rubberized fabrics, vulcanized rubber clothing, foam-rubber products, and miscellaneous rubber specialties. This group also includes establishments engaged in molding primary plastics for the trade and manufacturing miscellaneous finished plastic products.

The rubber industry makes a great variety of products, chief of which are tires for motor vehicles, aircraft, and farm machinery. The tire industry is big from the standpoint of scale of operations. In large-scale operations, the tire industry is superseded only by the steel and aircraft industries. Accounting for the large size of the production unit is the fact that mechanization at practically every stage in the process requires a huge amount of invested capital. The industry is oligopolistic dominated by the 'Big Four', B. F. Goodrich, Firestone, Goodyear, and U.S. Rubber. Table 4.4 does indicate that internal scale economies are an important contributor to total scale for establishments in this industry.

While we did not hypothesize a negative and significant sign for the localization economies variable (i.e., localization diseconomies) our statistical findings indicate just this result. This result can be explained, however, by the relatively large size of plant in this industry. The negative and significant sign for localization economies coupled with the positive and significant sign for internal scale economies implies that establishments in this industry are large enough to have internalized many of the traditional localization economies.

SIC 30 is also highly concentrated in metropolitan areas. For example, in 1963 the ratio of SMSA employment to total employment for this industry stood at 62.7%.[10] Our regression results show that urbanization economies (.0158002) offset somewhat by diseconomies (−.00024054) are an important component of total scale for establishments comprising this major grouping.

4.3.11. SIC 31 Leather and leather products

The leather industry converts hides and skins into leather. About 80% of its output is used in the manufacture of shoes. The remainder is used in the manufacture of gloves, belting, bags, harness, upholstery, bookbinding, etc.

The leather industry is a relatively small-scale industry. According to the Bureau of the Census in 1972 value added in the industry was only 2,870.5 million, which exceeded, slightly, SIC 21 tobacco manufacturing only. The major portion of the output, about 60%, consists of light leather, such as upper leather for shoes, gloves, garments, and fancy leather products. The remainder consists of heavy leather such as sole leather for shoes, for bags and luggage, and upholstery leather. Although at one time most tanneries produced a wide range of products, plants today tend to specialize on a basis of raw materials and finished products to such an extent that the industry has become divided into the heavy leather industry on the one hand, and the light industry on the other hand.

Our statistical results do indicate the importance of both urbanization economies (.0200125) and diseconomies (−.0004170). According to Hoover, due to the small scale of this industry, agglomeration 'in the leather industry must depend mainly upon advantages in access to specialized markets for materials, products, and supplies, in machinery servicing, and in the development of by-product industries.'[11] In addition, Hoover suggests that pecuniary diseconomies may operate since 'other factors . . . might work with labor costs to keep the leather industry out of larger urban centers. The group space required is relatively large, and the esthetic qualities of the tannery are low, so that rents and zoning laws could be expected to suburbanize or even ruralize the industry to some extent.'[12]

4.3.12. SIC 32 Stone, clay, and glass products

This major group includes establishments engaged in manufacturing flat glass and other glass products, cement, structural clay products, pottery, concrete and gypsum products, cut stone products, abrasive and asbestos products, etc., from resources taken primarily from the earth in the form of stone, clay and sand.

Our statistical results indicate the existence of internal diseconomies to scale for plants in this industry. In addition, our empirical results suggest that localization economies are an important contribution to total scale. Many establishments in this industry are concentrated in the northeast, especially Pennsylvania and Ohio. It is quite possible that the small size of plant, which typifies this industry, together with the high degree of concentration in the urbanized northeast accounts for the positive and significant sign on the localization economies variable. That is, economies of scale for establishments in stone, clay and glass are internalized at the industry level.

4.3.13. SIC 33 Primary metal industries

This group includes establishments engaged in the smelting and refining of ferrous and nonferrous metals from ore, pig, or scrap; in the rolling, drawing and alloying of ferrous and nonferrous metals; in the manufacture of casting, forgings, and other basic products of ferrous and nonferrous metals; and in the manufacture of nails, spikes, and insulated wire and cable.

Our regression results indicate the importance of internal scale economies in this industry. Here, we would have expected the large-scale compound to be the dominant source of scale. Large-scale operation, for both the firm and its plants, is the rule. The amount of capital necessary to engage in the manufacturing of iron and steel products is extremely large. Certain economies, which are technical in nature, come from increasing the size of an individual iron and steel plant. These technical economies are largely due to more efficient use of factors of production with respect to heating, shaping and moving the product.

Moreover, an integrated mill needs considerable space. The housing of massive machinery and equipment takes up much space. In addition, to assure continuity of operation a mill stores on its premises mountains of raw materials – iron ore, coke, coal and limestone. Not only is land an important input into the productive process, but it is land of a certain quality, i.e., near water to be used for cooling and transport. We have argued that the exhaustion of favorable land as concentration of population increases could show up as urbanization diseconomies. This may in part explain the negative and significant sign on the urbanization diseconomies proxy. Likewise, the products of primary metals are bulky and heavy and therefore require specialized handling and transport. Inasmuch as larger concentrations of population entail increased usage of transport resources, this could also help explain the presence of urbanization diseconomies for this industry.

Finally, we notice that the sign on the localization economies variable is negative and significant. This result can be explained, once again, by the relatively large size of establishment in this industry. The negative and significant sign for localization economies implies that the establishments in this industry are large enough to internalize many of the usual localization economies.

4.3.14. SIC 34 Fabricated metal products
This industry consists of establishments engaged in fabricating ferrous and nonferrous metal products such as metal cans, tinware, hand tools, cutlery, general hardware, nonelectrical heating apparatus, fabricated structural metal products, metal stamping and a variety of metal and wire products not elsewhere classified.

It is difficult to generalize about this industry, since the products are countless in number and infinitely varied in size, shape and purpose. It can be noted, however, that all the products in this grouping are composed principally of the metal produced by SIC 33.

Another broad generalization is that production processes for establishment in this industry are capital intensive. For example, the production process of the metal containers industry is highly automated. Continuous high-speed assembly lines characterize the industry. Turning to another important sub-industry under this classification, fabricated structural metal products, we find production processes which also require heavy use of machines.

Our empirical results indicate the presence of urbanization economies as well as urbanization diseconomies for establishments in this industry. One anomalous result is the negative and significant sign on the localization economies variable. In this instance the sign on the internal scale economies variable is not significantly different from zero.

4.3.15. SIC 35 Machinery, except electrical
Establishments under this classification are engaged in manufacturing machinery and equipment, other than electrical equipment

and transportation equipment.

The empirical results suggest the presence of internal diseconomies of scale for establishments in this industry. More importantly, our regression results indicate the existence of localization economies in this industry. This could be due to economies in the utilization of labor which develops in clusters. Labor costs account for anywhere from 35 to 65% of the total cost of machinery. The availability of skilled mechanical labor is therefore an important prerequisite to the production of machinery. Many kinds of machinery cannot be produced on a mass production basis, so large quantities of labor are required. Since skills are transferable from the production of some types of machines to others, different types of machinery producers are frequently located in the same metropolitan area. That is, each producer recognizes that he will be best able to find suitable labor in sufficient quantity when establishments in this industry tend to cluster.

4.3.16. SIC 36 Electrical machinery

This group includes establishments engaged in manufacturing machinery apparatus and supplies for the generation, storage, transmission, transformation and utilization of electrical energy. The manufacture of household appliances is also included in this group.

The empirical results for electrical machinery (SIC 36) are, not surprisingly, identical to the results obtained for machinery, except electrical (SIC 35). The rationale for the statistically significant coefficients is in this case the same as reported for SIC 35.

4.3.17. SIC 37 Transportation equipment

Important products produced by establishments classified in this major group include motor vehicles, aircraft, ships, boats, railroad equipment, and miscellaneous transportation equipment such as motorcycles, bicycles and horse drawn vehicles.

Our regression results failed to turn up any significant variables for the transportation equipment industry. On *a priori* grounds we might expect localization economies to be of some importance to establishments in this industry. The distribution of motor vehicle plants in the U.S. is well known. More than one-third of the value added is concentrated in Michigan, especially in Detroit and its environs. Parts-and-accessories-producing (SIC 3714) plants are located adjacent to automotive producing plants, but consist of small establishments utilizing a high value of labor inputs. External economies of scale result when a large concentration of units producing the same type of product and linked products locate in the same metropolitan areas. A division of labor develops in the linked industry, allowing plants to engage in the production of highly specialized outputs. These specialized plants, by supplying several firms with the same products, can both develop a high level of technical expertise and achieve some scale economies from the larger volume of output. Moreover, with large-scale concentration, a specialized labor force tends to develop.

Turning to the aircraft industry, a number of significant localization trends have occurred in recent years. For a long period of time there was a distinct separation of the assembly plants and the factories that produced engines, parts and propellers. The engine and parts plants are, however, increasingly attracted to the assembly plants. In addition, E. W. Miller (1970:64) has argued that the need for highly specialized technical know-how has become the greatest single factor accounting for intraindustry clustering of this activity.

4.3.18. SIC 38 Instruments and related products

This industry consists of establishments engaged in manufacturing mechanical measuring, engineering, laboratory and scientific research instruments; optical instruments and lenses; surgical, medical and dental instruments, equipment and supplies; ophthalmic goods; photographic equipment and supplies; and watches and clocks.

This industry is among the newest and most rapidly growing of American industries. The industry is strongly oriented to areas where people possess scientific knowledge. Major manufacturing belts have developed near Harvard and the Massachusetts Institute of Technology, California Institute of Technology and U.C.L.A. and at Stanford and the University of California at Berkeley. Indeed, the personnel in this industry is so highly specialized, that intraindustry clustering may be necessary to ensure that sufficient quantity and quality of labor exists.

As our empirical results suggest, localization economies dominate for establishments comprising this industry (a coefficient of 17.8694 for this variable). Our statistical results also indicate negative returns to increasing the size of the average plant (i.e., a coefficient of -7.76459 for the internal scale economies proxy).

4.3.19. SIC 39 Miscellaneous manufacturing

As the heading indicates, this group includes establishments primarily engaged in manufacturing products not classified elsewhere. Industries in this group fall into the following categories: jewelry, silverware and plated ware; musical instruments; toys; sporting and athletic goods; pens, pencils, and other office and artists' materials; buttons, costume novelties, miscellaneous notions, brooms and brushes; morticians' goods, etc.

It is hard to generalize about establishments in this industry, since the products are countless in number and infinitely varied. Generally, however, establishments included in this grouping tend to be small in scale. As our theory suggests, small-scale plants are unable to exploit economies resulting primarily from indivisibilities internally, and, as a result, are drawn to metropolitan areas. Our empirical results lend credibility to this point of view. Table 4.4 indicates that urbanization economies (a coefficient of .0171128), offset somewhat by diseconomies of concentration (a coefficient of −.0002637), are important elements in an interpretation of scale economies for plants in this industry.

4.4. GENERALIZATION OF THE EMPIRICAL RESULTS

The empirical evidence which we have just described suggests that there are important economies of scale in many industries. Some broad conclusions about these economies for manufacturing activity do emerge.

While the internal scale economies variable was significantly different from zero for 7 of the 19 industries studied, it was positive and significant in only 3 instances (i.e., for only 15% of the cases). This result can be compared to the finding that localization economies are positive and significant for 5 of the 19 industries studied (i.e., 26% of the cases) and that urbanization economies are positive and significant for 12 out of the 19 industries comprising this study (or for 63% of the cases). This comparison reveals the overwhelming importance of external economies as a contributor to total scale in manufacturing. The empirical results lend support to the underlying hypothesis of this work — that agglomeration economies are of paramount importance for an understanding of the forces leading to concentration of production in comparatively few urbanized or central places in the United States.

Finally, we must point out that the goodness of fit statistics, R^2's, are quite impressive considering the level of aggregation involved and the fact that this is a cross-sectional model. All-in-all, we have obtained considerable support for the approach taken to measurement and decomposition of the agglomeration phenomenon in manufacturing.

NOTES

1. Data for the years 1957, 1959–1962, 1964–1966 and 1969–1971 are taken from *Annual Census of Manufactures: Area Studies*, various reports. Data for the years 1958, 1963, 1967, and 1972 are taken from the *Census of Manufactures: Area Studies*, various reports.
2. The Bureau of Labor Statistics provides wholesale price indices for the two-digit SIC classifications. These indices were employed to convert both payroll and wages into real terms.
3. Two sources were utilized. *The Census of Manufactures: Area Studies*, various reports, provides data on the number of establishments for the years 1958, 1963, 1967, and 1972. For the interim years data are taken from *County Business Patterns*, various reports.
4. Ideally we would like to conduct this test for all of the SMSA comprising this study. However, just to carry out this test for a single SMSA requires an extreme amount of data and time (which was believed could be more productively spent elsewhere in the study). In addition, it is believed that the overall results for one SMSA could be generalized. As such, the Boton SMSA was chosen since it contained data for most of the industries employed in this study.
5. Tables 4.1a–4.1s of Carlino (1976) give complete statistics for all industries.
6. In addition, population per square mile of land area for both the SMSA as a whole and its suburban ring were tried. In general, these population density proxies did not work nearly as well as population scale. Data for the population scale variable were obtained from U.S. Bureau of the Census, 1970 Census of Population and Housing, PIIC (2), *General Demographic Trends for Metropolitan Areas*, 1960 to 1970.
7. Alderfer and Michl (1957:342–343).
8. Mills (1972:17).
9. Ibid., p. 17.
10. Ibid., p. 17.
11. Hoover (1937:123).
12. Ibid., p. 123.

5. Conclusion

The primary purpose of this study is the extension of empirically validated knowledge regarding the importance of the various agglomeration forces on manufacturing activity. Prior research in this field has been either too aggregative (i.e., indiscriminately combining large-scale, localization and urbanization economies in a single measure) or isolating only on one of the components of scale. To this author's knowledge, this study is the first to estimate the scale coefficient by manufacturing industrial classification across SMSA's. In addition, this work is unique in that we are able to decompose a more direct measure of scale for the various manufacturing industries located in metropolitan areas. This decomposition provides insight into which combination of the internal and external economies, as well as diseconomies, of large-scale production and/or clustering, seems to be important for an understanding of the industry-by-industry profile of agglomeration.

Moreover, the empirical analysis of the last chapter has important implications for regional or metropolitan development and growth. The tendency of economic activity to concentrate in cities in the United States has been persistent and increasing. Despite considerable disamenities such as pollution and congestion on the one hand, and pecuniary diseconomies on the other, metropolitan places have witnessed the fastest growth of economic activity.

For manufacturing activity the locational pull of metropolitan areas has taken an increased weight due to the external economies available therein. As transport cost and resource or material orientation have declined in importance, agglomeration economies have therefore become an increasing determinate in the locational matrix of plants. The production of goods has been rationalized by dividing the production process into sequences of individual operations. This increase in the number of steps or stages in the production process has reduced the importance of material orientation as a locational factor by reducing the fraction of economic activity which is tied to specific resource deposits. This tendency has been reinforced by technological change which reduces dependence on specific resource deposits. That is, not only has technical change increased the number of steps in production, it has also tended to decrease the importance of specific raw material sites by creating alternatives. This could be due to increased factor substitution in a given production process, or a completely new process may develop, or even an entirely new product may be introduced.

Furthermore, innovation in transportation has steadily reduced the relative cost of overcoming distance. In the presence of agglomeration economies found in cities this reduction in transport cost orientation has a centralizing effect on manufacturing activity.

In sum, the importance of agglomeration economies found in cities has increased considerably as fewer manufacturing units remain concerned with the processing of material and as technological innovation in transport steadily reduces transportation cost to the firm.

This increased locational pull of agglomeration economies has important implications for location decision-makers of firms. Agglomeration economies express themselves through lower average cost of production and conceptually their spatial variations could be treated in the same fashion as any other item of cost. Thus, location decision-makers need information regarding the external economies offered to their industry by various metropolitan areas in order to know which is the optimal location for a proposed new plant or expansion. Moreover, since the physical plant and equipment of firms exhibits considerable inertia, firms pay a penalty for suboptimal locations over the long-run and therefore are motivated to seek optimal sites.

Knowledge of agglomeration economies has important implications not only for location decision-makers of firms but for city and regional planning authorities as well. The results of our cross-sectional regression model indicate the importance of agglomeration economies in an explanation of total scale for most industries. This information could be used in the formulation of regional or area development strategy by local, state or federal planners. As our cross-sectional empirical results reveal, urbanization economies seem to be important to plants in many industries. As such, one highly plausible area development prescription is to develop the urban infrastructure (e.g., specialized business services, financial intermediaries, etc.) first, and the rest should follow.

In general, any attempt on the part of a planning agency, at any level, to influence plant location presupposes knowledge of the nature and operation of the variables which determine locational choice. As agglomeration economies become an increasingly more important locational variable, operational models, such as the one presented in the last two chapters, should be of considerable assistance to planners as they formulate industrial development strategy in a spatial context.

Finally, as hinted at above, urban growth could be viewed as an agglomeration process. Bergsman, Greenston and Healy (1972:263) argue that firms find it profitable to cluster together geographically with firms in their own and other industries. For some activities, however, large cities may offer more diseconomies than economies. Thus we can view urban growth as continual agglomeration and deglomeration of economic activities, responding to external economies and diseconomies created by previous location decisions of firms and individuals. The last point suggests a possible extension of the present work. The Dhrymes specification is a constant elasticity of substitution production function. As such, it, or the standard CES form, might be used in future research as a tool for testing whether there are significant metropolitan differences in the elasticity of substitution for a given industry. Such an investigation would enable us to gain information about metropolitan differences in the growth potential of manufacturing activities.

In concluding this chapter we might point out a few limitations of the empirical approach. In conducting production function analysis it is necessary to make certain simplifying assumptions: simplications such as perfect competition, the two-input case and homogeneity of degree one. In addition, problems such as capacity utilization, indivisibilities, the short-run versus the long-run, dynamic aspects, etc., are usually by-passed. In this study, we have dealt more realistically with many of these points, since we assume imperfect competition and homogeneity of degree h, account for dynamic aspects, albeit in a crude fashion, and address ourselves to the long-run versus the short-run aspect, etc. A basic limitation of any applied production function analysis, especially in regional research, is the failure to account for land. Furthermore, the homogeneous factor assumption is even more suspect for regional purposes since capital and labour are different, just because they occupy different locations. As we saw, our model is capable of incorporating technical change, provided that it is of the disembodied variety. But this is more an assumption made for convenience, and we discussed how it could have effected our statistical results in those industries where embodied technical progress is the rule.

Furthermore, the cross-sectional and time-series regression models are subject to several questions about specification. The specification of a regression model consists of a formulation of the regression equation and of statements or assumptions concerning the regressors and the disturbance term. Thus a specification error occurs if either the formulation of the regression equation or one of the underlying assumptions is incorrect. Several kinds of specification errors could be mentioned with respect to the empirical analysis. First, there is the possibility of omitting a relevant explanatory variable. An example here might be the omission of land from the production function. Second, there is the possibility of inclusion of an irrelevant variable in the cross-sectional model. Third, there is the possibility of incorrectly specifying the mathematical form of the regression equation. This possibility was considered with respect to the cross-sectional regression model. Rather than assuming a linear functional form, we attempted to test for it. The Box-Cox transformation is a non-linear technique, which makes the linear specification a testable hypothesis. A prerequisite for conducting the test, however, is convergence of the generalized Box-Cox form. Unfortunately, convergence of our Box-Cox equation was not obtained for any industry comprised in this study. Finally, we could incorrectly specify the way in which the disturbances enter the regression equation (e.g., we assume that the disturbances enter into the non-linear production function in a multiplicative fashion).

The consequences of committing these various types of specification errors are well known. Most econometric textbooks deal with them extensively. Generally, with the exception of the case of including irrelevant explanatory variables in the regression equation, all the specification errors that we have considered lead to biasness and inconsistency of the least squares estimators. In the case of including irrelevant explanatory variables, the least squares estimators are unbiased and consistent but not efficient.

While these qualifications are serious in their own right, they must be placed in perspective. Indeed, there is little pretence that the foregoing analysis provides an exhaustive solution to the measurement problem. This work does establish, however, that production function analysis is a most fruitful method of inquiry into the measurement of agglomeration economies. These qualifications are mentioned rather to suggest possible avenues of future research.

Appendix A

The purpose of this appendix is to demonstrate formally several propositions of Chapter 3. Namely, that the CES-like production function given by equation (3.8), generates equation (3.9). In addition, we will demonstrate that by assuming that only the first marginal condition holds, equation (3.6a) of Chapter 3, ensures that the short-run and long-run optimization problem is identical.

The Dhrymes CES-like production function can be written

$$Q = C(t)[\alpha_1(t)K^{h\delta} + \alpha_2(t)L^{h\delta}]^{1/\delta} \tag{A1}$$

Let $Z = [\alpha_1(t)K^{h\delta} + \alpha_2(t)L^{h\delta}]$, then

$$Q = C(t)Z^{1/\delta} \tag{A2}$$

Differentiation of (A2) with respect to labor yields:

$$\frac{\partial Q}{\partial L} = 1/\delta C(t)Z^{(1/\delta)-1}h\delta\alpha_2(t)L^{h\delta-1} \tag{A2'}$$

$$= 1/\delta C(t)(Z^{1/\delta})^{(1-\delta)}h\delta\alpha_2(t)L^{h\delta-1}$$

Substituting in for Z

$$\frac{\partial Q}{\partial L} = 1/\delta Q^{(1-\delta)}h\delta\alpha_2(t)L^{h\delta-1}[C(t)]^\delta \tag{A3}$$

Using the following relationships given by Dhrymes

$$\frac{\partial Q}{\partial L} = W\left(\frac{1+\epsilon}{1+\eta}\right), \quad \alpha(t) = \frac{1+\epsilon}{1+\eta}$$

implies:

$$\frac{\partial Q}{\partial L} = W\alpha(t)$$

Substituting into (A3):

$$W\alpha(t) = 1/\delta \; Q^{(1-\delta)} h \delta \alpha_2(t) L^{h\delta-1} [C_3(\alpha_1(t))^{-1/\delta}]^\delta \tag{A4}$$

where

$$C(t) = C_3[\alpha_1(t)]^{-1/\delta}$$

Rearranging (A4) becomes

$$W\alpha(t) = 1/\delta \; Q^{(1-\delta)} h \delta L^{h\delta-1} C_3 \left(\frac{\alpha_2(t)}{\alpha_1(t)} \right) \tag{A5}$$

Now $\alpha_1(t) + \alpha_2(t) = 1$, thus (A5) can be written

$$W\alpha(t) = 1/\delta \; Q^{(1-\delta)} h \delta L^{h\delta-1} C_3 \left[\frac{1 - \alpha_1(t)}{\alpha_1(t)} \right]$$

$$= 1/\delta \; Q^{(1-\delta)} h \delta L^{h\delta-1} C_3 \left(\frac{1}{\alpha_1(t)} - 1 \right)$$

$$\alpha_1 = \frac{h}{h + C_2 A \alpha(t)},$$

so

$$W\alpha(t) = 1/\delta Q^{(1-\delta)} h \delta L^{h\delta-1} C_3^\delta \frac{h + C_2 A \alpha(t)}{h} - 1$$

$$= h Q^{(1-\delta)} L^{h\delta-1} C_3^\delta \frac{C_2 A \alpha(t)}{h}$$

Dividing through by $\alpha(t)$ and rearranging:

$$W = h Q^{(1-\delta)} L^{h\delta-1} C_3^\delta \left[\frac{C_2 A}{h} \right]$$

Now $C_3 = C_2^{-1/\delta}$ so

APPENDIX A

$$W = hQ^{(1-\delta)}L^{h\delta-1}(C_2^{-1/\delta})^\delta \frac{C_2 A}{h}$$

$$= A Q^{(1-\delta)} L^{h\delta-1}$$

Letting $\beta = 1 - \delta$ and $\gamma = h\delta - 1$:

$$W = AQ^\beta L^\gamma \tag{A6}$$

Thus, a production function like (A1) leads to a Cobb-Douglas type relation between wages, output and labor (A6). Since the scale coefficient is given by

$$h = \frac{1+\gamma}{1-\beta} \tag{A7}$$

which is determined by equation (A6) and since equation (A6) is free from technical change, we will have a 'pure' scale measure in equation (A7) provided that technical change is of the disembodied variety. One question still not answered is whether or not one can derive a production which is homogeneous of degree h in capital and labor, which in turn leads to a relationship like (A6), which in turn leads to a pure scale measure, if technical change is assumed to be embodied.

Notice that equation (A6), which is our estimating equation, was derived from the production function (A1) by 'optimizing' with respect to labor while capital was *free* to vary, i.e., equation (A2'). To demonstrate that the long-run (capital free to vary) and short-run (capital stock constant) are the same, differentiate (A2) totally:

$$dQ = \left[1/\delta C(t) Z^{(1/\delta)-(\delta/\delta)} h\delta \alpha_2(t) L^{h-1}\right] dL +$$

$$\left[1/\delta C(t) Z^{(1/\delta)-(\delta/\delta)} h\delta \alpha_1(t) K^{h\delta-1}\right] dK$$

If the capital stock is constant this implies that $dK = 0$, thus

$$dQ = \left[1/\delta C(t) Z^{(1/\delta)-(\delta/\delta)} h\delta \alpha_2(t) L^{h\delta-1}\right] dL$$

or dividing through by dL

$$dQ/dL = 1/\delta\, C(t) Z^{(1/\delta)-(\delta/\delta)} h\delta \alpha_2(t) L^{h\delta-1} \qquad (A8)$$

Notice that the right hand sides of equation (A2′) and (A8) are identical. Thus, letting the capital stock be free to vary equation (A2′) or hold the capital stock constant (A8) yields an identical first-order condition for profit maximation. In addition, either equations (A2′) or (A8) can be rearranged to yield:

$$W = A Q^\beta L^\gamma$$

our estimating equation used to derive the scale parameter as

$$h = \frac{1+\gamma}{1-\beta}$$

which is itself independent of the level of the capital stock.

Appendix B

STANDARD METROPOLITAN STATISTICAL AREAS

Akron
Albany
Allentown
Anaheim
Atlanta
Baltimore
Birmingham
Boston
Bridgeport
Buffalo
Canton
Chattanooga
Chicago
Chicago-Consolidated Areas
Cincinnati
Cleveland
Columbus
Dallas
Davenport
Dayton
Denver
Detroit
Fort Worth
Gary
Grand Rapids
Greensboro
Greenville
Hartford
Houston
Indianapolis
Jersey City
Kansas City
Lancaster
Los Angeles
Louisville
Memphis
Milwaukee
Minneapolis
Nashville
Newark
New Orleans
New York
New York-Consolidated Areas
Paterson
Peoria
Philadelphia
Phoenix
Pittsburgh
Portland
Providence
Reading
Richmond
Rochester
Rockford
St. Louis
San Diego
San Francisco
San Jose
Seattle
Springfield
Syracuse
Toledo
Utica-Rome
Wichita
Wilkes-Barre
Worcester
York
Youngstown

References

Alderfer, E. B., Michl, H. E. *Economics of American Industry*, New York: McGraw-Hill, (1957).

Alonso, W. 'The Economics of Urban Size', *Papers and Proceedings of the Regional Science Association*, Vol. 27, (1971), pp. 67–83.

Arrow, K. J., Chenery, H. B., Minhas, B. S., and Solow, R. M. 'Capital Labor Substitution and Economic Efficiency', *The Review of Economics and Statistics*, Vol. 43, (1961), pp. 225–234, 246–268.

Bain, J. S. 'Economies of Scale, Concentration, and Entry', *American Economic Review*, Vol. XLIV, (1954), pp. 15–39.

Baumol, W. J. 'Macroeconomics of Unbalanced Growth: the Anatomy of Urban Crisis', *American Economic Review*, Vol. 57, (1967), pp. 415–26.

Bergsman, J., Greenston, P. and Healy, R. 'The Agglomeration Process in Urban Growth', *Urban Studies*, Vol. 9, (1972), pp. 263–288.

Bopp, R. and Gordon, P. 'Agglomeration Economies and Industrial Economic Linkages: Comment", *Journal of Regional Science*, Vol. 17 (1977), pp. 125–26.

Borukhov, E. 'On the Urban Agglomeration and Economic Efficiency: Comment', *Economic Development and Cultural Change*, Vol. 24, (1975), pp. 199–205.

Bos, H. C. *Spatial Dispersion of Economic Activity*, North-Holland: Rotterdam University Press, (1965).

Carlino, G. A. 'Agglomeration of Manufacturing Activity in Metropolitan Areas: Theory and Management". Unpublished Ph.D. dissertation, University of Pittsburgh, (1976).

Chinitz, B. 'Contrasts in Agglomeration: New York and Pittsburgh', *American Economic Review*, Papers, Vol. 51, (1961), pp. 279–289.

Christaller, W. *Central Places in Southern Germany*, Trans. by C. W. Baskin, Englewood Cliffs, N.J.: Prentice-Hall, (1966).

Clemente, F. and Sturgis, R. B. 'Population Size and Industrial Diversification', *Urban Studies*, Vol. 8, (1971), pp. 65–68.

Dhrymes, P. J. "Some Extensions and Tests for the CES Class of Production Functions', *The Review of Economics and Statistics*, Vol. XLVII, (1965), pp. 357–366.

Dhrymes, P. J. *Econometrics: Statistical Foundations and Applications*, New York: Harper and Row, (1970).

Edel, M. 'Land Values and the Costs of Urban Congestion: Measurement and Distribution', in Ecole Paratique des Hautes Etudes, VIe Section, *Political Economy of Environment: Problems of Method*, The Hague: Mouton, (1972), pp. 61–90.

Edwards, R. C., Reich, M., and Weisskopf, T. E. *The Capitalist System: A Radical Analysis of American Society*, Englewood Cliffs, N.J.: Prentice-Hall, (1972).

Evans, A. W. 'The Pure Theory of City Size in an Industrial Economy', *Urban Studies*, Vol. 9, (1972), pp. 49–77.

Ferguson, C. E. 'Substitution, Technical Progress, and Returns to Scale', *American Economic Review*, Proceedings, (1965), pp. 296–305.

Ferguson, C. E. *The Neoclassical Theory of Production and Distribution*, Cambridge, England: Cambridge University Press, (1969).

REFERENCES

Fuchs, V. R. 'Differentials in Hourly Earnings by Region and City Size', *National Bureau of Economic Research*, Occasional Paper 101, (1967).

Garofalo, G. A. 'A Theoretical and Empirical Investigation into the Effects of Agglomeration Forces on Urban Industrial Growth', Unpublished Ph.D. dissertation, University of Pittsburgh, (1974).

Greenhut, M. L. *Plant Location in Theory and in Practice*, Chapel Hill: The University of North Carolina Press, 1956.

Greenhut, M. L. *Microeconomics and the Space Economy*, Chicago: Scott Foresman and Company, (1963).

Greenhut, M. L. *A Theory of the Firm in Economic Space*, New York: Appleton-Century-Crofts, (1970).

Greenhut, M. L., Hwang, M., and Ohta, H. 'Observations on the Shape and Relevance of the Spatial Demand Function', *Econometrica*, Vol. 43, (1975), pp. 669–82.

Griliches, Z. 'Hybrid Corn: An Exploration in the Economics of Technological Change', *Econometrica*, Vol. 25, (1957), pp. 501–522.

Griliches, Z. 'Production Function in Manufacturing: Some Preliminary Results', in M. Brown, (ed), *The Theory and Empirical Analysis of Production*, National Bureau of Economic Research, New York: Columbia University Press, (1967), pp. 275–322.

Griliches, Z. and Ringstad, V. *Economies of Scale and the Form of the Production Function: An Econometric Study of Norwegian Manufacturing Establishment Data*, Amsterdam: North-Holland Publishing Company, (1971).

Gunnarson, J. *Production Systems and Hierarchies of Centers*, Studies in Applied Regional Science, Vol. 7, Leiden: Martinus Nijhoff Social Sciences Division, (1977).

Guthrie, J. A. 'Economies of Scale and Regional Development', *Papers and Proceedings of the Regional Science Association*, Vol. I, (1955), pp. J1–J10.

Hagerstrand, T. *The Propagation of Innovation Waves*, Lund Studies in Geography, Series B. Human Geography, No. 4, (1952).

Hagerstrand, T. 'Aspects of the Spatial Structure of Social Communication and the Diffusion of Information', *Papers and Proceedings of the Regional Science Association*, Vol. 16, (1966), pp. 27–42.

Hagerstrand, T. *Innovation Diffusion as a Spatial Process*, Trans. A. Pred, Chicago: University of Chicago Press.

Hansen, G. C. and Laing, N. F., (eds.), *Capital and Growth*, Baltimore: Penguin Books, (1971).

Harcourt, G. C. *Some Cambridge Controversies in the Theory of Capital*, Cambridge, England: Cambridge University Press, (1972).

Harris, C. C. and Hopkins, F. E., *Locational Analysis*, Lexington, Mass, Health Lexington Books, (1972).

Harris, J. R. and Wheeler, D. 'Agglomeration Economies: Theory and Measurement', Paper presented at the Urban Economics Conference, Keele, England, (July 1971).

Hoch, I. 'Income and City Size', *Urban Studies*, Vol. 9, (1972), pp. 299–328.

Hoover, E. M. *Location Theory and the Shoe and Leather Industries*, Cambridge, Mass: Harvard University Press, (1937).

Hoover, E. M. *The Location of Economic Activity*, New York: McGraw-Hill, (1948).

Hoover, E. M. *An Introduction to Regional Economics*, New York: Alfred A. Knopf, Inc, (1971).

Isard, W. *Location and Space Economy*, Cambridge, Mass: The MIT Press, (1956).

Isard, W., and Smith, T. E. 'Location Games: With Application to Classic Location Problems', *Papers and Proceedings of the Regional Science Association*, Vol. 19, (1967), pp. 45–80.

REFERENCES

Isard, W. *Introduction to Regional Science*, Englewood Cliffs, N.J.: Prentice-Hall, Inc., (1975).

Johnson, J. *Econometric Models*, New York: McGraw-Hill, (1960).

Kaldor, N. 'The Equilibrium of the Firm', *Economic Journal*, Vol. 44, (1934).

Kawashima, T. 'Urban Agglomeration Economies in Manufacturing Industries', *Regional Science Association Papers and Proceedings*, Vol. 34, (1975), pp. 157–175.

Kendall, M. G. and Sturat, A. *The Advanced Theory of Statistics*, Vol. 1, London: C. Griffin and Co. Limited, (1967).

Kmenta, *Elements of Econometrics*, New York: The Macmillan Company, (1971).

Koopmann, T. C. *Three Essays on the State of Economic Science*, New York: McGraw-Hill, (1957).

Koopmann, T. C. and Bechmann, "Assignment Problems and the Location of Economic Activity', in M. Edel and J. Rothenberg's, *Readings in Urban Economics*, New York: Macmillan Company, (1972).

Kuznets, S. *Population Redistribution and Economic Growth, United States, 1870–1950: III: Demographic Analysis and Interrelations*, The American Philosophical Society, Philadelphia, (1964).

Lampard, E. E. 'The History of Cities in Economically Advanced Areas', *Economic Development and Cultural Change*, Vol. 3, (1954–55), pp. 81–136.

Latham, W. R. *Locational Behavior in Manufacturing Industry*, Studies in Applied Regional Science, Vol. 4, Leiden: Martinus Nijhoff Social Sciences Division, (1976).

Lave, L. B. 'Congestion and Urban Location', *Papers and Proceedings of the Regional Science Association*, Vol. 25, (1970), pp. 133–149.

Lichtenberg, R. M. *One-Tenth of a Nation*, Cambridge, Mass: Harvard University Press for the Regional Plan Association, (1960).

Lösch, A. 'The Nature of Economic Regions', *Southern Economic Journal*, Vol. 5, (1938), pp. 71–78.

Lösch, A. *The Economics of Location*, Trans. W. F. Stolper and W. H. Woglom, New Haven: Yale University Press, (1954).

Maeshiro, A. 'A Primer to Econometrics: The Essentials of Inferential Statistics', Unpublished manuscript, University of Pittsburgh, (1973).

Mansfield, E. *The Economies of Technical Change*, New York: W. W. Norton, (1968).

Marcus, M. 'Agglomeration Economies: A Suggested Approach', *Land Economies*, Vol. 41, (1965), pp. 279–84.

Marshall, A. *Principles of Economics*, 8th edition, London: Macmillan and Company, (1966).

Meade, J. E. 'External Economies and Diseconomies in a Competitive Situation', *Economic Journal*, Vol. LXII, (1952), pp. 54–67.

Mera, K. 'On the Urban Agglomeration and Economic Efficiency', *Economic Development and Cultural Change*, Vol. 21, (1973), pp. 309–24.

Miller, E. W. *A Geography of Industrial Location*, Dubuque, Iowa: Wm. C. Brown Company, (1970).

Mills, E. S. *Studies in the Structure of the Urban Economy*, Baltimore: Johns Hopkins Press, (1972a).

Mills, E. S. 'An Aggregative Model of Resource Allocation in a Metropolitan Area', in M. Edel and J. Rothenberg's, *Readings in Urban Economics*, New York: The Macmillan Company, (1972b).

Moses, L. N. 'Location and the Theory of Production', *Quarterly Journal of Economics*, Vol. 72, (1958), pp. 259–272.

Nelson, R. R. 'Aggregate Production Functions', *American Economic Review*, Vol. LIV, (1964), pp. 576–606.

REFERENCES

Nerlove, M. 'Recent Empirical Studies of CES and Related Production Functions', in M. Brown (ed.), *The Theory and Empirical Analysis of Production*, National Bureau of Economic Research, New York: Columbia University Press, (1967), pp. 55–122.

Ohlin, B. *Interregional and International Trade*, Cambridge, Mass: Harvard University Press, (1967).

Paelinck, J. H. and Nijkamp, P. *Operational Theory and Method in Regional Economics*, Lexington: Heath and Company, (1975).

Parr, J. B. and Denike, K. G. 'Theoretical Problems in Central Place Analysis', *Economic Geography*, Vol. 44, (1970), pp. 568–586.

Patterson, C. F. *Economies of Scale in Manufacturing Industry*, Cambridge, England: The Cambridge University Press, (1971).

Pred, A. R. *The Spatial Dynamics of U.S. Urban-Industrial Growth, 1800–1914*, Cambridge, Mass: the MIT Press, (1966).

Puryear, D. L. 'Central Place Theory and Interurban Specialization', Unpublished Ph.D. dissertation, Princeton University, (1973).

Rasmussen, R. W. *Urban Economics*, New York: Harper and Row, (1973).

Richardson, H. W. *Elements of Regional Economics*, Baltimore: Penguin Books, (1969).

Richardson, H. W. *Regional Growth Theory*, New York: Halsted Press, (1973a).

Richardson, H. W. *The Economics of Urban Size*, Westmead, England: Saxon House, (1973b).

Richter, C. E. 'The Impact of Industrial Linkages on Geographic Association', *Journal of Regional Science*, Vol. 9, (1969), pp. 19–28.

Robinson, E. A. G. *The Structure of Competitive Industry*, Chicago: The University of Chicago Press, (1962).

Robinson, J. 'The Production Function and the Theory of Capital', *Review of Economic Studies*, Vol. 21, (1953–4), pp. 81–106.

Rocca, C. A. 'Productivity in Brazilian Manufacturing', Appendix 2 of Joel Bergsman's, *Brazil: Industrialization and Trade Policies*, Cambridge, England: Oxford University Press.

Segal, D. 'Are There Returns to Scale in City Size', *Review of Economics and Statistics*, Vol. 58, (1976), pp. 339–50.

Segal, D. *Urban Economics*, Homewood: Richard D. Irwin, Inc., (1977).

Shefer, D. 'Returns to Scale and Elasticities of Substitution by Size of Establishment for Two-Digit U.S. Manufacturing Industries – 1958–1963', Discussion Paper Series No. 26, Regional Science Research Institute, Philadelphia, Pennsylvania, (1969).

Shefer, D. 'Localization Economies in SMSAs: A Production Function Analysis', *Journal of Regional Science*, Vol. 13, (1973), pp. 55–64.

Siebert, H. *Regional Economic Growth: Theory and Policy*, Scranton, Pennsylvania: International Textbook Co., (1969).

Silberston, A. 'Economies of Scale in Theory and Practice', *Economic Journal*, Vol. 82, (1972), pp. 369–91.

Solow, R. M. 'Technical Change and the Aggregate Production Function', *Review of Economics and Statistics*, Vol. 49, (1957).

Solow, R. M. 'Technical Progress, Capital Formation, and Economic Growth', *American Economic Review*, Vol. LII, (1962), pp. 76–78.

Smith, D. M. *Industrial Location: An Economic Geographical Analysis*, New York, John Wiley and Sons, Inc., (1971).

Stanback, T. M., and Knight, R. V. *The Metropolitan Economy*, New York: Columbia University Press, (1970).

Stevens, B. 'An Application of Game Theory to Problems in Location Strategy', *Papers and Proceedings of the Regional Science Association*, Vol. 19, (1967), pp. 45–80.

Streit, M. E. 'Spatial Associations and Economic Linkages Between Industries', *Journal of Regional Science*, Vol. 9, (1969), pp. 117–188.

Streit, M. E. 'Agglomeration Economies and Industrial Linkages: A Reply', *Journal of Regional Studies*, Vol. 17, (1977), pp. 129–30.

Struyk, R. J. 'Spatial Concentration of Manufacturing Employment in Metropolitan Areas: Some Empirical Evidence", *Economic Geography*, Vol. 48, (1972), pp. 189–92.

Sveikauskas, L. 'The Productivity of Cities', *Quarterly Journal of Economics*, Vol. 89, (1975), pp. 393–413.

Technical Committee on Industrial Classification, *Standard Industrial Classification Manual*, Washington, D.C.: GPO, (1957).

Thoman, R. S. and Corbin, P. B. *The Geography of Economic Activity*, New York: McGraw-Hill, (1974).

Thompson, W. R. *A Preface to Urban Economics*, Resources for the Future, Baltimore: Johns Hopkins Press, (1965).

Thurow, L. C. and Taylor, L. D. 'The Interaction Between the Actual and Potential Rates of Growth', *Review of Economics and Statistics*, Vol. XLVIII, (1966), pp. 351–360.

Tybout, R. A. and Mattila, J. M. 'Agglomeration of Manufacturing in Detroit', *Journal of Regional Science*, Vol. 17, (1977), pp. 1–16.

Ullman, E. L. 'The Nature of Cities Reconsidered', *Papers and Proceedings of the Regional Science Association*, Vol. 9, (1962), pp. 7–23.

U.S. Bureau of the Census, 1970 Census of Population and Housing, PIIC (2), *General Demographic Trends for Metropolitan Areas, 1960 to 1970*.

U.S. Department of Commerce, Bureau of Census, *Annual Census of Manufacturing, 1957, 1959–62, 1964–66, and 1969–71*, Washington, D.C.: GPO.

U.S. Department of Commerce, Bureau of Census, *Census of Manufacturing: Area Studies, 1958, 1963, 1967 and 1972*, Washington, D.C.: GPO.

U.S. Department of Commerce, Bureau of Census, *County Business Patterns*, Various Years, Washington, D.C.: GPO.

U.S. Department of Commerce, Office of Business Economics, *Business Conditions Digest*, Washington, D.C.: GPO (1972).

U.S. Department of Labor, Bureau of Labor Statistics, *Monthly Labor Review*, Washington, D.C.: GPO, various issues.

Vernon, R. *Metropolis 1985*, Cambridge, Mass: Harvard University Press, 1960.

von Böventer, E. G. 'Optimal Spatial Structure and Regional Development', *Kyklos*, Vol. 23, (1970), pp. 903–24.

Webber, M. J. *Impact of Uncertainty on Location*, Cambridge, Mass: The MIT Press, (1972).

Webber, A. Alfred Weber's *Theory of the Location of Industries*, Trans. C. J. Friedrich, Chicago: University of Chicago Press, (1929).

Williamson, J. G. and Swanson, J. A. 'The Growth of Cities in the American Northeast, 1820–1970', *Explorations in Entrepreneurial History* (Supplement), Vol. 4, (1966), pp. 1–101.

Studies in applied regional science

Vol. 1
On the use of input-output models for regional planning
W. A. Schaffer (Ed.)

ISBN 90 207 0626 8

Vol. 2
Forecasting transportation impacts upon land use
P. F. Wendt (Ed.)

ISBN 90 207 0627 6

Vol. 3
Estimation of stochastic input-output models
S. D. Gerking

ISBN 90 207 0628 4

Vol. 4
Locational behavior in manufacturing industries
William R. Latham III

ISBN 90 207 0638 1

Martinus Nijhoff Social Sciences Division Leiden 1976

Vol. 5
Regional economic structure and environmental pollution
B.E.M.G. Coupé

This book deals with the ever-increasing problem of pollution. The author has constructed an extensive interregional model for economic activities and pollution. Each region has its own internal structure, expressed by means of intersectoral commodity flows, investments, employment, consumption and pollution. In addition, interregional linkages are taken into account.
Coupé's two-region model (applied to some Dutch provinces) is used to calculate an equilibrium in terms of production and pollution abatement. The solution procedure is based on a programming model. The model aims at supplying a means of fighting pollution and managing the environment, with a view to guiding the regions to an acceptable life level.

ISBN 90 207 0646 2

Vol. 6
The demand for urban water
P. Darr, S. L. Feldman, C. Kamen

Because the urban water industry remained relatively impervious to veneral inflationary trends until the early 1970's tariff design and water demand forecasting played a relatively minor role in utility management. General shortages in supply were often abetted by capacity additions designed using common engineering practice. However, the range of choice for water management can include adjustments to remedy disequilibria through management of the demand side of the market.
This volume explores the components affecting demands using combined economic, engineering and social psychological tools and recommends remedies in tariff design to conform to basic economic postulates.

ISBN 90 207 0647 0

Vol. 7
Production systems and hierarchies of centres
J. Gunnarsson

In this study hierarchies of centres are discussed, with special references to Tingergen-Bos systems. The author also uses component analysis to examine whether the structure of the Swedish system of centres resembles the structure of different hierarchy models.

The author constructs models, for instance, a mixed-integer programming model. Relations between regularities for optimal systems (the size-distribution of centres and space-functional relations between types of centres) and input-output coefficients as well as the location of natural resources are studied. A quadratic programming model is also proposed. This extension of the problem makes it possible to determine capacities of plants and systems of centres simultaneously. Thus, distribution of plant sizes and city sizes may be studied in the same model.

Implications of the theory of entrepreneurial behaviour are also investigated.

ISBN 90 207 0688 8

Vol. 8
Multi-criteria analysis and regional decision-making
A. van Delft and P. Nijkamp

The study focuses on the use of multi-criteria methods as a tool for adequate decision-making. After a discussion of traditional evaluation techniques (cost-benefit analysis, for instance) several multi-criteria decision methods are reviewed. Particular attention is paid to 'concordance analysis' as it is called. Several variants of this new evaluation method are developed.

The second part of the study describes an empirical application of concordance analysis to regional industrialization policy, viz. a new industrial marine complex near the Rhine delta in the Netherlands. The operational aspects of concordance analysis are highlighted particularly in the case of conflicting views on regional growth and environmental protection.

ISBN 90 207 0689 6

Vol. 9
Economic aspects of regional welfare
C. P. A. Bartels

This study is focused on the analysis of relationships between various economic aspects of regional welfare, especially income distribution and unemployment. A wide variety of methodological questions are explored, with a particular emphasis on their empirical relevance.

The first part of the book is devoted to methods for describing income distributions concisely and exploring characteristics of regional unemployment series. Alternative ways of defining income inequality measures are considered, with a special emphasis on a full explicit integration of normative and positive elements in this definition.

Characteristics of unemployment series are also empirically explored, using several statistical techniques. A new frequency domain technique, i.e. principal component analysis of spectral estimates, is applied to the regional data.

In the second part of the book, a link is made between income and employment based on an explanatory analysis. Empirical relations are estimated for regional income and its distribution, using several socio-economic explanatory variables, and the study concludes with the presentation of a scheme for an integrated regional labor market/income.

ISBN 90 207 0706 X

Vol. 10
Spatial representation and spatial interaction
Ian Masser and P. J. B. Brown

This book is directed towards regional scientists, geographers, urban, regional and transport planners and others with a particular interest in the practical application of methods of spatial analysis. In recent years, the problem of spatial representation has been recognized as being of fundamental importance to the effective application of a wide range of analytical methods. This book draws together for the first time various related pieces of work undertaken in the field of spatial interaction research and sets them in a general framework within which the problem of spatial representation is viewed as part of the general problem of aggregation. Two kinds of strategy for dealing with this problem in relation to interaction data are outlined in an introductory overview of the field and their practical application is illustrated in subsequent chapters. In the concluding chapter, a number of general themes from the various streams of work are identified and a number of areas defined for further investigation.

ISBN 90 207 0717.5

Vol. 11
Tourism and regional growth
Moheb Ghali, editor

Tourism plays a major role in Hawaii's economy. Policies designed to control the rate of growth of tourism will, therefore, affect the growth paths of the economy. This book is the first systematic empirical study of the growth operations open to a region.

The first part is devoted to studying regional growth under resource constraints. This is followed by the study of the region's major exports, their determinants and projections of their future growth. An econometric model of regional growth is presented in the third part, and is utilized to simulate the growth paths of income, employment, migration and unemployment under alternative tourism policies. In the last part of the book, the fiscal implications of the alternative growth paths are derived.

ISBN 90 207 0716 7